Jane Austen's Guide to Good Relationships

Jane Austen's Guide to Good Relationships

Ronald W. Richardson

Ronald W. Richardson, Tucson, Arizona. Published 2017.
©2017 Ronald W. Richardson

ISBN-13: 978-1541114623
ISBN-10: 1541114620

Cover design and interior illustrations: Amy Haagsma
Cover photo: Ronald W. Richardson
Copy editing: Eva van Emden

For more books by Ronald Richardson, see his author page at https://www.amazon.com/Ronald-W.-Richard son/e/B001JS10P6.

Acknowledgments

This book is a tribute to two of my heroes: novelist Jane Austen (died 1817) and professor of psychiatry Dr. Murray Bowen (died 1990). Both of these people closely observed how human beings function in their relationships and drew similar conclusions about what can make relationships problematic and what can make them better. For a long time, I have wanted to write a popular book on relationships that shows the connection between these two thinkers. Here it is.

I want to thank my wife, Lois, for suggesting that I read Austen. I thank all of those people who are working to further the understanding of Bowen theory and its application to a number of areas of human life. I thank my editor, Eva van Emden, who made my writing more understandable. In addition, I thank Amy Haagsma for her cover design, the interior artwork, and family diagrams.

We each have a whole colony in us, you know.

Pablo Picasso

Table of Contents

Introduction: Jane Austen and Good Relationships Today   1

1 Starting Where Austen Started   15

2 The Ties That Bind Are Emotional   31

3 Watching Our Systems in Action   43

4 Anxiety Can Really Upset an Emotional System   61

5 Must We Bless the Ties That Bind?   81

6 Closeness and Distance in Relationships   95

7 Reacting to Our Differences   109

8 The Sibling Relationship and Good Relationships   127

9 The Key to Making Good Relationships   141

10 How Relationships Can Get Really Complicated: Triangles   159

11 Your Relationships Can Improve   181

Appendix I   A Brief Biography of Jane Austen   199

Appendix II   Jane Austen's Family   201

Appendix III   Family Diagrams for Each Novel   203

Appendix IIII   Counseling and Training Opportunities   209

Introduction

Jane Austen and Good Relationships Today

Really? Jane Austen? A woman who died two hundred years ago in 1817? What can she tell us about relationships today? Our world is so different from hers.

When we read her books, her characters speak in what almost seems like a foreign language. No one talks that way today. And the romantic relations between men and women back then were so restricted that we become frustrated with what her characters can do and say when courting.

The very word "courtship" seems foreign to our ears. We never hear young men now say they are "courting" a young woman. Of course, there was nothing like social media and online dating. We have new kinds of families now with gay marriage, unheard of in her day. And casual sex hookups, while they clearly happened in her time (Austen even obliquely writes about a few), were never openly acknowledged as they are today.

On the other hand, many of us enjoy Austen's language and read her for her wit and humor. She was a master of irony. People in her day recognized her as an excellent author. Even royalty loved to read her. Her approach to the novel and her characterization were innovative and fascinating. In fact, she was the first truly "psychological" writer, leading the way for many authors up to the present day.

But enough about her literary legacy. Personally, Jane Austen was not, as we might assume, all "prim and proper." She was a gossip within her circle of family and close friends. In her private letters to her closest friend, her older sister Cassandra, she said some outrageous things about neighbors and acquaintances. Once, speaking of a husband and wife at a party, she wrote to Cassandra, **"I was as civil to them as their bad breath would allow."**

She loved to go out and socialize with friends and neighbors and to have fun. She went to almost every neighborhood ball that she could. She loved dancing, which by the way, was about the only acceptable way that men and women could touch each other physically. She wrote to her sister once about what could have been her version of getting her groove on, "I am almost afraid to tell you how my Irish friend and I behaved. Imagine to yourself everything most profligate and shocking in the way of dancing and sitting down together."

We laugh at this, but after hearing about their growing closeness, her friend's family brought him back to Ireland because it was clear that he and Jane were getting "too close." Just like in her novels, they thought she was not in the right social class for him. He eventually became the Chief Justice of the Supreme Court of Ireland. He confessed his love for her when he was in his nineties, long after she had died.

Austen's time differs from ours in many ways, but her novels portray men and women who struggle with the same passions we have, and who have the same questions about a possible partner: Is he (or she) the one? What is love anyway? Do I want to spend my life with this person? Could it work between him (or her) and me? Dare I risk investing myself in this relationship? Can I commit to this person?

And what about this business of "dating" today anyway? For many of us—especially for people who have been married and are now divorced—it is a challenging endeavor. Dating is hard work; it can be dispiriting and even humiliating. How do we present ourselves to others? Filling out a profile on a dating site can make us feel like a commodity to be sold to the highest bidder. What is the "image" we want to market? How truthful should we be?

On the positive side, today, unlike in Austen's day, women don't need men to rescue them or support them financially. Men and women can be true equals in their relationships.

What we have in common with Jane Austen's heroes is that we still have the same romantic feelings, and these impel us to look for loving relationships. Many of us grew up on fairy tales about princes and princesses falling in love. Even today, Disney and Pixar produce stories like this. These universal, crazy-in-love feelings are a part of our physical and psychological makeup. They are thrilling to experience. Normally, these intense feelings burn out after a couple of years, but we can replace them with a deep and abiding love that is more profound and long lasting. Austen knew about this.

A Therapist's Perspective

Good relationships have been the focus of my professional life as well as a personal goal. I was the executive director of a large, city-wide counseling agency in Vancouver, Canada. I had a staff of twenty-five clinicians. Professionally, I saw firsthand the kind of messes we can make of our relational life, and how we can sort them out and make them better.

Personally, becoming someone capable of having decent relationships has taken me a lot of time. I have made my own messes and had to endure some painful experiences in the process. Growing up, I was an only child living with a single mother who moved around a lot. We moved five times in my first six years of school. Because I was always dropped into new settings, my social skills developed slowly. Like many only children, I could be happy just playing by myself. Not good training for being married. In the seventh grade, after a move from Missouri to Hollywood, California, I began to make lasting friendships. I still keep in touch with several of my good friends from that time, even though we now live in different parts of North America.

When I started dating early in high school, I was a jerk. When I was no longer interested in a girl, I just disappeared on her. I felt guilty, but I was ignorant and didn't know what else to do. Austen describes some young men like me, like John Thorpe in *Northanger Abbey*. Later, in college, I fell seriously in love with a young woman and wanted to marry her. Since she features later in this book, I will call her June. I was still not good at being a loving and interested person. I did not know how to be open about myself, or express tender feelings. When June broke off the relationship, partly for these reasons, I was devastated.

After that, **I started to think I might never get married.** Having been a "singleton" all my life, that did not seem awful to me. Then I met Lois and fell in love with her. After six months, we got married. However, I was not any better at relating to someone I cared about. I was anxious about getting close. We learned early on (like on the honeymoon) that love does not "conquer all." We probably had more conflict in our relationship than most couples, but we loved each other enough to keep working at it.

We had some counseling that helped us to stay together, but things did not change for us significantly. One thing the counseling did was help me decide to become a therapist myself. After I became a marriage and family therapist—probably to work on myself as much as anything—I discovered the therapeutic approach outlined in this book. We began to use it for ourselves, and then things began to change for us. This does not mean the approach is easy or that we got better at our relationship quickly. **This approach is not a quick fix solution for relationships.** Like a GPS, it clarifies the way to get there, but getting there takes work. Austen knew this, and she shows how her characters did their work. Lois and I celebrate our fiftieth year of marriage in 2017. This therapeutic approach, developed by Dr. Murray Bowen, is called family systems theory. Dr. Bowen became a hero for me.

How I Learned to Love Jane Austen

I discovered Jane Austen in 1985, in a bookstore in England. Lois and I were spending a year traveling through Europe in a Volkswagen camping van. Yes, it was wonderful. Amazingly, we did just fine in that tiny space together for a year. We were doing better together by this time. In England, looking for books to take with us over to the Continent, Lois said to me, "Here, read this." I said, **"Oh that's Jane Austen. I don't want to read her."** Lois said, "Really! Read it. I think you'll like it." Even though I had been an English literature major in university, I had avoided anything to do with Austen. Probably the main reason was that she didn't fit in with my self-image as a "guy." Also, I didn't understand irony when I was a young man. I didn't see her relevance to my life, and I was not interested in her.

Dutifully and not too happily, that night I started reading *Sense and Sensibility*. Almost immediately, I got excited. I kept saying to Lois, "She's got it! She's really got it! Here, listen to this . . ." I read passage after passage out loud, unable to believe I had never known anything about this woman or her work. I was excited that **she thought about relationships in much the same way I did as a therapist**. She gave case examples in her novels of the kind of theory that guided my

6

therapy work with people. She quickly became my literary hero. Thank you, Lois. Thank you, Jane.

I began to think about how to share my enthusiasm about Jane Austen's relationship insights in a therapy context as a popular book. In 2008, I published *Becoming Your Best: A Self-Help Guide for Thinking People.* Along with (heavily disguised) examples from my clinical practice, I used examples from Austen's novels. Still, I wanted to do a book that focused on Austen and relationships, and thus you have this book.

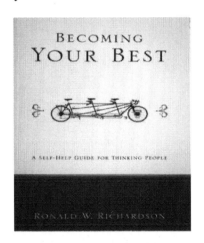

What This Book Is About

This book is not about the wonderful romantic feelings, or the powerful sexual attraction that we feel toward potential partners. It is not advice on the art of dating. Nor is it a book on communication skills. Plenty of other books have covered these aspects of relationships. Austen well knew that on top of these skills, there is something else involved in having good, lasting relationships, and that is our character, the kind of person we are. She believed we need a strong sense of self (not selfishness), of who we are, and that this strong self is a means by which we could know others. It is our touchstone. When Elizabeth Bennet in *Pride and Prejudice* finally sees clearly the character of the two men in her life, she exclaims in horror that she had not known herself. Her lack of knowledge of her own character had kept her from knowing them.

Austen was interested in whether a person is reliable, trustworthy, truthful, open instead of secretive, respectful, and consistent in living out these virtues. To know this, we have to know ourselves and have these qualities ourselves. For her, these underlying aspects of an emotionally mature person were what made for good character personally and for good relationships with others.

Few of us enter adulthood with these qualities in place. We develop a strong self over the years, and that is hard work. Part of how we do it is in getting to know others, watching them, and watching how we are with them. However, I agree with Austen that this hard work is how we build a happy life. Whether we remain single or eventually get married, this sense of self is at the core of our happiness.

This book is about all of the things that can get in the way of developing this strong sense of self and creating good relationships. We may not think about these things much, but they are central to a satisfying relational life.

We accept a much wider variety of relationships than the people of Jane Austen's time, yet we continue to focus on the same questions she did. Research shows that most people, young and old, straight and gay, are looking for a long-term partner. The more permanent and mature that relationship, the better (for most of us). The question is how do we make that relationship the best it can be? **A significant amount of our happiness in life depends on how good our relationships are.** In my marital therapy work, this central issue concerned every client of mine. Regardless of our material station in life, learning to love and be loved, having truly close and committed life partners, is a major goal in life.

Most social research finds that the more good relationships we have, the healthier we will be. And this is true for physical health, not just psychological health. Love truly is a matter of the heart—the actual physical heart. People with good relational lives have fewer heart attacks and live longer. When our relational lives are good, we feel good: we feel energized and happy regardless of the material circumstances of our lives. When any of our close relationships go badly, not only do we feel emotionally devastated, it affects us physically. Austen shows us this in *Sense and Sensibility* when Marianne Dashwood almost dies after Willoughby rejects her.

As you read this book, you will find that **Jane Austen really did know something about what makes for good relationships.** She knew how to develop them and keep them, and what was hurtful and damaging. She addressed all kinds of relationship questions. How do we relate to our family? Can we be close to them when we find them embarrassing, or difficult to get along with? Can we be close to them and still be ourselves? How can we find and have truly good friends? We can even apply these principles to creating better relationships in our workplace.

Bowen Family Systems Theory

The approach that I describe in this book is Bowen family systems theory—Bowen theory for short. Lois and I used it to improve our relationship, and I based practically all of the therapy I provided in my clinical practice on this approach. Many marriage and family therapists worldwide use this approach. While I will not describe the theory in full detail, I think the parts I do describe will be useful to you, in all of your relationships.

Dr. Murray Bowen was a professor of psychiatry at Georgetown University in Washington, D.C. He received grants from the National Institute of Mental Health to hospitalize whole families who had a schizophrenic member. He put together a research team who observed these families twenty-four hours per day for several years, and from these observations, he began to develop the concepts in his theory of how people function in relationships.

He was able to apply these observations to patients with less severe, more common problems. Then, in a truly revolutionary way, he applied his concepts to his own life and relationships, including his workplace. **His approach is not about what to do to others to change them, but how to be with others in order to make things better.** Bowen theory is about all human beings in all cultures. Underneath our cultural facades, humans are all much the same. Students from each of the world's continents have come to my training programs for therapists, and they all say, "This theory works in my culture."

Jane Austen, of course, did not know about family systems theory, but she was an excellent observer of how people function in relationships, and especially what they need to do to make their relationships better. Since Bowen theory developed by observing how people actually function in their relationships, there are many parallels in their ways of seeing. Austen's ideas about human relationships are very close to Bowen theory.

The best authors are excellent observers of human functioning. They watch how people behave in their close relationships and write about it. This is what strikes us as "true" in their fiction. Authors with great literary skills, like Jane Austen, also entertain us with their well-written descriptions about people and their relationships.

Bowen Theory Is the Guide; Austen Gives Us the Examples

In each chapter, I introduce and develop some key aspect of Bowen theory. Unlike in my previous book on Austen, I will not give examples from my clinical work. Instead, I will show how Austen illustrates the various concepts in her novels.

It would be easy for me to load this book up with Austen quotes and references that support my points, but if I did, the book would be four times as long, so I keep these to a minimum. Throughout the narrative, I also intersperse stories of how the theory has worked for me personally. I hope my personal story adds a note of authenticity to what I am saying and does not get in your way. Each chapter ends with a few questions for you to ponder with regard to your own life and relationships. It is a good idea to discuss these questions with partners and friends.

Austen's novels focus primarily on the process of finding a marital partner, what I call the "marriage project." The movie versions of her books tend to focus almost exclusively on this aspect of her novels, without doing justice to the other serious topics that underlie this story line. I don't focus on the romantic love aspect of finding a partner as much as what the partners bring to that powerful and thrilling experience from their own emotional history.

With all of this as an introduction, let's remember the names of Austen's six published novels: *Northanger Abbey, Sense and Sensibility, Pride and Prejudice, Mansfield Park, Emma,* and her last book, *Persuasion.* Because page numbers vary in the many different editions of her books, quotes from them will only give the chapter numbers. Austen divided her books into volumes, restarting the chapter numbers with each volume. I will not give volume numbers but will use the ordinal numbering system for all of the chapters, as most modern editions of her books do.

Spoiler Alert

I have two further caveats. First, I do assume that you the reader are somewhat familiar with Austen's novels. But if you're not, you will still grasp the point of what I am saying. I hope that what I have to say will stimulate you to read, or re-read, her novels and will increase your enjoyment when you do.

Second, while making my points I sometimes give away the outcome of the story. But much of the delight in reading Austen is not for the suspense about whether the characters "live happily ever after" (here is the spoiler: in each case they do); the pleasure is in the way she tells her stories and the language she uses.

For those of you who are not familiar with Austen, I have given a brief biography in Appendix I.

1

Starting Where Austen Started

Three or four families in a country village is the very thing to work on.

Jane Austen

We developed our relational habits growing up in our family. The epigram above comes from a letter Austen wrote to her niece, who also wanted to become a novelist. It tells us what Austen considered her topic to be. It is different from the way many people read her books. Her stories are not just about the particular female heroes and their love lives. **Each one of Austen's novels begins by introducing us to the hero's family.** Both Jane Austen and Murray Bowen see the family that people grow up in as a major factor in what kind of people they become and what kind of relationships they will have as adults.

This is not necessarily good news for many readers. Many people spend their adult years trying to get away from their families. I did as a young man. I put three thousand miles between my mother and me. As grown-up men and women, we like to think we are more autonomous, or independent, or free from family influence. Other people acknowledge the influence of family and, at the same time, blame them for how they are, saying, "They screwed up my life." A few people idealize their family and try to recreate it in their adult lives. Each of these stances toward the family brings its own set of problems to our adult relationships.

The Family of Origin

Therapists call our birth family the family of origin, as opposed to the family of creation, which is composed of our own partners and children. One of the first things I do as I start working with clients, no matter what problem brings them in, is to draw a family of origin diagram. This diagram shows who was in the person's family as they were growing up.

Below is a passage from one of Austen's earliest novels, *Northanger Abbey*. First, I will show you a simple family diagram for the main hero of that book, Catherine Morland. (By the way, in Appendix III, I give the family diagrams for all six novels.)

In a family diagram, males are represented as squares and females are circles. (Some people see this as quite appropriate.) Mr. and Mrs. Morland were Cathe-

16

rine's parents. The horizontal line between them represents their marriage. Austen gives us his first name (Richard) but not hers. Their children are on the vertical lines coming down from their marriage line. The oldest child is at the left end (in this case James) and progresses toward the right end with the youngest child, whose name and sex (along with seven other siblings) we are not given. Catherine was the fourth of ten children. We only know the name of two of her siblings (James, her oldest brother, and Sally, the sister born after Catherine) and the sex of the two other older brothers born between her and James. Also, we know that Catherine was eighteen years old at the time of our story and her younger sister was seventeen.

The Morland Family

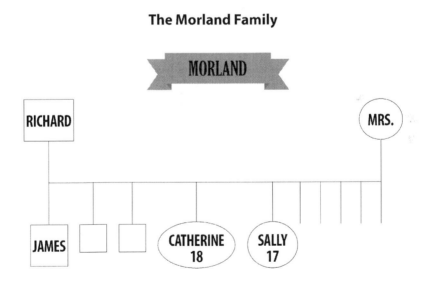

By the way, having ten children was a normal size family in Austen's times. Often it took two or three wives to get there because they died in giving birth. Austen remarks on this in the passage below. Here is a selection from the opening lines of *Northanger Abbey*, starting with page 1 of chapter 1.

No one who had ever seen Catherine Morland in her infancy would have supposed her born to be an heroine. Her situation in life, the character of her father and mother, her own person and disposition, were all equally against her. . . .

[Her father] was not in the least addicted to locking up his daughters. Her mother was a woman of useful plain sense, with a good temper, and, what is more remarkable, with a good constitution. She had three sons before Catherine was born; and instead of dying in bringing the latter into the world, as anybody might expect, she still lived on—lived to have six children more—to see them growing up around her, and to enjoy excellent health herself. . . .

[Catherine] was fond of all boy's plays, and greatly preferred cricket not merely to dolls, but to the more heroic enjoyments of infancy, nursing a dormouse, feeding a canary-bird, or watering a rosebush. . . . She was moreover noisy and wild, hated confinement and cleanliness, and loved nothing so well in the world as rolling down the green slope at the back of the house. . . .

Mrs. Morland was a very good woman, and wished to see her children everything they ought to be; but her time was so much occupied in lying-in [related to pregnancy and giving birth] and teaching the little ones, that her elder daughters were inevitably left to shift for themselves; and it was not very wonderful that Catherine, who had by nature nothing heroic about her, should prefer cricket, baseball, riding on horseback, and running about the country at the age of fourteen, to books—or at least books of information—for, provided that nothing like useful knowledge could be gained from them, provided they were all story and no reflection, she had never any objection to books at all. But from fifteen to seventeen she was in training for a heroine; she read all such works as heroines must read to supply their memories with those quotations which are so serviceable and so soothing in the vicissitudes of their eventful lives.

Austen tells us about Catherine's family and how she got to be the kind of tomboy she is and how relatively uninformed she is about life in general. As a younger sister of brothers, she is oriented to men and most men will likely be attracted to her. Her parents have been very lenient and allowed her to remain ignorant of many things. At the age of fifteen, she started reading gothic romance novels, which were all the rage then. These were usually horror novels with characters and situations that bore little resemblance to real life. Catherine, with so little guidance from her parents, had no reason to know how unrealistic they were. Later in this novel, she succumbs to imagining she is actually living in one of these stories. Austen is telling us what kind of young woman, from what kind of family, could get herself into the kind of situations described in this novel and have these kinds of relational difficulties.

Northanger Abbey is Austen's parody of gothic novels. She was making fun of them and of the kind of people who read them and believed them to be realistic. Catherine is a sympathetic character, but her ignorance of real life and how relationships work gets her into trouble frequently. She is lucky to find a caring and considerate man (Henry Tilney) at one of the dances in Bath who is attracted to her and wants to help guide her education in life and relationships.

In Austen's novels, family relationships play a major role in the story right through to the end. That is part of what draws me to her novels. Austen always gives the family context of her characters, and she shows us the inner experience of her characters. We hear them attempting to think things through, and we understand their feelings. Much of this inner experience connects with their outer family life.

In my case, growing up only with my mom and never seeing a husband and wife interacting up close, I had no models of marriage to either adopt or rebel against. My mom and I kept a lot of distance from each other. She also, like Catherine's mother, was a very permissive parent, and we never even fought or argued. I didn't learn anything about dealing with differences or conflict in close relationships. Like Catherine, **I was ignorant of many things**.

When I married, I expected to have the kind of relationship I had with my mother: somewhat distant, doing mostly what I wanted, and refusing to talk about any disagreements. Lois came from quite a different kind of family. Her family was more intensely close, and they did argue over their differences. That was the expectation she brought to our marriage. It became clear early in the marriage that my way of relating was not going to fly if I wanted to keep it. It took me a long time to get comfortable dealing with the closeness, the differences, and the conflict in marriage. I thoroughly enjoyed all of the rest of it!

The Family as a System

Dr. Bowen focused on the family as a system. Each family member is a part of that system. Traditional psychotherapy focused just on the individual patient and the person's inner subjective experience of thoughts and feelings. Family was not a central focus. In fact, it was taboo for a therapist to talk with the actual family members of a patient. Bowen saw that our inner subjective experiences and feelings connect to our outer, more objective, actual family relationships. **To understand our feelings better, we have to understand our family better.** The subjective territory of feelings does not tell the whole story about who we are. What people actually do in managing their lives with one another is observable, objective hard data.

What is a system? It is a group of interrelated parts. There is a reciprocity between the interconnected parts of a larger whole. A car is a mechanical system. All of the parts, working together, are what makes the car go. If an essential part is broken or missing, the car won't move, at least not correctly or safely. **In a system, the functioning of one part ties in to the functioning of other parts**.

Our body is a living system. Each part has its own function, but that functioning is affected by that of the other parts. If the lungs are not getting enough air, the heart has to work harder to get oxygen into the blood-stream. If one part of the body is failing, then other parts are affected as well. Our physical body is a system that works to keep a healthy functional equilibrium or balance (homeostasis) among the various parts.

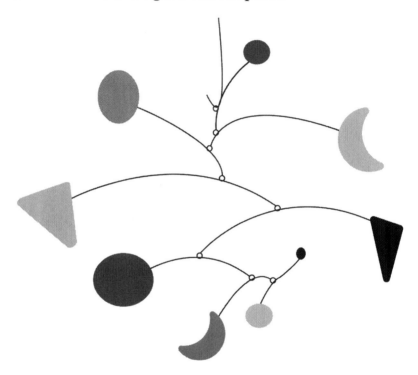

I like to think of the family system as a delicately bal-anced mobile like the one pictured above. Each part in a mobile exists in relation to the other parts. **When one part of the mobile moves, all of the other parts move in response**. This mobile is a simple system compared to the family system.

If you take away any part of this mobile, the balance of the whole is affected. In a living system like a family, this happens when one member marries or moves away, or there is a divorce or a death. The family as a whole gets out of balance, and it has to work hard to adjust and rebalance itself. It has to find a new equilibrium.

Austen shows this in *Emma*. The Woodhouse family has to adjust to many losses, and this affects Emma's own life. In *Sense and Sensibility*, the family system is disrupted when old Mr. Dashwood dies. In *Persuasion*, the Elliot family is displaced when their income is lowered and they lose the family estate. In every case, these changes affect the emotional lives of the individuals in the family.

If a new person is added to the family system through birth or marriage, or there is an affair (even if no one else knows about it), then adjustments in the balance have to be made. When the life circumstances or status of one member change, as with the first year of school or a graduation for a child; a job promotion, demotion, layoff, or retirement for an adult; or a major debilitating illness, the other family members all have to adjust to the change. Each family manages these transitions with greater or lesser success.

Emotionality in the Human System

Emotionality is a primary factor in human relationship systems. We are very sensitive to the feelings in other people that we are close to, and we are very reactive to them. Jane Austen shows this clearly in her novels. Other family members influence her heroes. Not only that, other families influence them as well ("three or four families"). In addition, don't forget the even larger context of "the country village." Whether we grow up in the north, south, east or west of our country makes a difference in who we are. All levels of the system play their part in who we are and what we bring to our relationships.

Look again at *Northanger Abbey* and the two other main families that Catherine is involved with (see all three families in the diagram below). She is torn between the Thorpe family and the Tilney family, both of which impinge on her emotionally. She is deeply affected by their two influences and deciding which one to lean toward and away from.

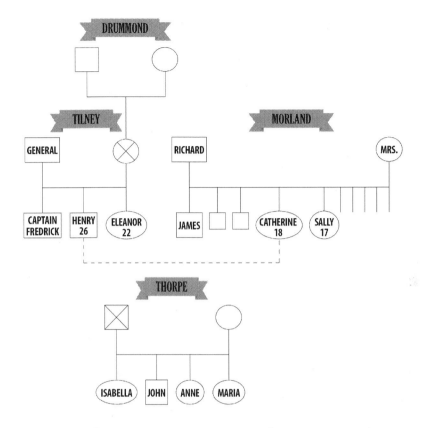

Given the many years we spend growing up in our families, it is normal for them to affect how we are as adults. It is not just the traumatic events of family life that have an impact on us. **It is the daily, repetitious interactions of family life that affect and shape us the most.** Current research in the study of the brain shows just how much this is the case. The psychologist Louis Cozolino has said in the introduction to his book *The Neuroscience of Human Relationships: Attachment and the Developing Social Brain*:

Humans exist within a paradox: We conceive of ourselves as individuals yet spend our lives embedded in relationships that build, shape, and influence our brains. . . . Yet, while we are busy cherishing our individuality, our brains and minds are being stimulated, influenced, and regulated by those around us. . . . Gradually, we are discovering that we are social creatures with brains and minds that are part of larger organisms called families, communities, and cultures. . . . This awareness is making it increasingly clear that to understand a person, we need to look beyond the individual. . . . The brain is a social organ of adaptation built through interactions with others. . . . There are no single human brains—brains only exist within networks of other brains.

We connect to each other in an emotional network. As a simple example, you may be able to think of some situation today in which your feelings have been stirred up. If someone is upset with you about something you did, it is normal for you to be upset in response. The character of your response to their upset will then affect how they further respond to you. This is how we can get into fights with each other, or it is how we get into a loving mood.

Jane Austen was very clear about this reciprocal interconnection between people. Part of her genius is to be one of the first fiction writers not only to let us in on the character's inner life, but to show how that inner experience and the actions of one person affects others and vice versa. That is a system.

In a family, it is as if we are all connected to each other by rubber bands. Some of the bands are long and loose. Mr. Morland, in *Northanger Abbey*, is like this. He is not inclined to "locking up his daughters," unlike many fathers in that day. He is not a control freak. Mrs. Morland is an easygoing mother. She has few expectations of her children, and they are able to do as they please. The downside of this is that Catherine has little guidance in managing her relationships.

Some rubber bands connecting us to others in the system can be short and very taut. People connected by these bands will be highly sensitive to each other. They can feel the tension building through the tight bands. When one person moves, the taut rubber band will yank on others. In some cases, people become wary with each other. They are always alert, watching for some sign of difficulty, some anxiety, or some pull on the band, and they are ready to react with either a defensive or an offensive move. When this kind of stance goes on for many years, through repeated daily interactions, everyone involved is affected. That tension itself becomes a part of our personality. These sensitivities become a part of who we are. These experiences become neural pathways, as Cozolino says, encoded in our brains and we carry these into our ways of relating in adult relationships.

Over time, say the twenty years involved in living with and growing up in a family, the emotional patterns we develop to deal with each other in the family system become automatic. We will not even know they are a part of us. We think they are normal. **We are like fish that have no sense of what water is.** These patterns do not only affect our adult relationships, but they also affect our worldview and create what seems like "reality" to us.

We are not usually aware of how we are with others and what our impact on them is. We say we are "just being ourselves." Others may find us to be strange or funny, irritating or perhaps endearing (think of how Henry Tilney sees Catherine in *Northanger Abbey*). When two people come together, like in a marriage, or as they grow to become close friends, this business of "just being myself" may begin to affect the relationship. We may think that we ourselves are normal but the other person is strange. I thought Lois was abnormal for always wanting to talk things out because that was never a part of my family experience. It does not occur to us that there may be something odd or unpleasant about us. We think the other person is the problem.

The Individual Model

Most theories of psychotherapy base their approach on the individual model. This model diagnoses the individual person's problem and then proceeds to treat that problem without reference to how it ties in to the larger system. Most of us also approach our relationships with the individual model in operation. In *Pride and Prejudice*, both Elizabeth and Darcy diagnose each other according to the individual model in their first encounters. Neither one sees the emotional attitudes (the water they swim in) they themselves are bringing to those encounters, attitudes that developed in their own families. **They each focus only on the pride, or the rudeness, or arro-**

28

gance of the other without seeing themselves with the other.

Using the individual model is the reason so many highly knowledgeable and skilled people, even psychotherapists, still get in trouble in their own relational lives. The divorce rate among therapists is high. Many individual-model therapists have diagnosed their parents as the problem for their own lives, and although they are experts at their individual-model theories, these theories don't reveal to them the underlying, automatic, probably unconscious, assumptions they developed in their families. Their expertise leads them to diagnose others (including their own partners) rather than to see their own self and their own way of functioning in the context of their own family. And so they miss an important avenue toward making things better.

Darcy's maturity allows him, eventually, to see how he is affecting Elizabeth, and he is able to change his more arrogant and rude stance. He sees how he has been contributing to her reaction to him. She has a similar revelation about how she has been functioning with him. As each takes responsibility for how they are with the other, their relationship improves.

Part of what attracted me to Bowen theory was that it really helped me understand my way of functioning in relationships. It helped me with my wife, in my family of origin, and particularly with my mother. It helped me learn how to be different in those relationships and how to focus more on my way of relating rather than focusing on them and what I might have seen as their "bad" behavior. Things got immensely better as a result.

Questions to Ponder

At the end of each chapter, I give a few questions to ponder. The intent is to further stimulate your own thinking about issues raised in the chapter. You may think about them yourself, but I also recommend discussing them with a partner or a close friend. Some people even belong to reading groups where they discuss these questions.

1. What do you think are the strengths and weaknesses in the relationships that you developed in your family?

2. Are there particular people in your family of origin who you had taut-rubber-band relations with and those that you had looser relationships with?

3. Who were you closest to and most distant from in your family of origin growing up? Did those patterns ever change? How?

4. Can you see how your family of origin experience, and how you functioned in it, is affecting how you are in your relationships now?

2

The Ties That Bind Are
Emotional

**We cannot destroy kindred: our chains stretch a
little sometimes, but they never break.**
Marie de Sévigné

In both Bowen theory and Jane Austen's books, families
are not just systems; they are emotional systems. An
emotional system is all of the interconnected relationships plus the emotions of the participants. **You could
think of emotions as the energy and the relationships as the arena.** Together they create the drama of
family life, as well as the extra-family relationships that
we experience with others. Fiction writers create their
stories out of these basic ingredients.

In *Mansfield Park* (chapters 18 and 19), Sir Thomas
Bertram returns from his West Indies trip to find the
household rehearsing a play, and a morally questionable

one at that. On top of that, they are rearranging and decorating his private library as the stage for the play. He is angry. When he enters the house, the family knows immediately that he will be upset, and they in turn become highly agitated. **Austen describes how the emotional system of that household goes into a tailspin.**

In all of Austen's books, the primary focus of each family's emotional system is the marriage project for the family's daughters. It is the central drama for her heroes because most women at that time had no independent source of money. If they did, upon getting married, it became the husband's money to do with as he pleased. There were very few options for upper-class women to have jobs or work outside of the home. If a woman did not marry, and if her family could not support her (which is what Austen's brothers did for the Austen women after their father died), her options were to become either a governess or a prostitute. Both of these were nearly equally unacceptable. The idea of becoming a governess is part of what makes Jane Fairfax so depressed in *Emma*. She has no parents or family to support her.

I can give you an immediate example of the emotional system at work right now, as you read this book. You may start having some reactions to what I say, or how I present Jane Austen or Murray Bowen, and a certain level of emotional energy or intensity could develop around that. Here is one thing that could already stir you up. I have been using a term that may have offended some of you in talking about Austen's novels. You may have noticed that instead of saying "heroine," I use the term "hero" for Austen's female protagonists. I understand that some people may object to this, especially since Austen herself said "heroine," but for me, a character like Elizabeth Bennet is a hero.

Here is my rationale. I dislike the more passive and submissive connotation of "heroine." It tends to stir up associations of a woman being rescued by a man. We now say "author" or "actor," when referring to both sexes, and we use other gender-neutral terms for both men and women. We don't call the military women who now die in battle "heroines." When women started entering various artistic and professional fields, the male world did not fully appreciate them. These women were placed in a separate category by adding a suffix like "ess" to the name of what they were. To my ear, this has a diminutive effect, implying that the achievement is less because the person is a woman. I agree with Maya Angelou who said, **"She is not a sculptress, poetess, authoress. . . . A rose by any other name may smell as sweet, but a woman called by a devaluing name will only be weakened by the misnomer."**

So even if you get my rationale, and maybe even if you agree, it can still be hard to change your language. You could become critical of me. You might already be working on arguments to counter my argument. This is a small fragment, depending on the intensity of feeling involved, of an emotional system. Some of you will have a reaction each time I use the term. If we have face-to-face contact, as I have done when teaching this material to groups, our emotional systems will be activated. That is normal. It is the emotion plus the minimal relationship we have here as author and reader that creates our system.

Symptoms of Emotional System Difficulties

When two or more people are close over time (as happens in marriages and families of course, but also with friends and work associates), their emotionality intertwines and their feelings often intensify around some differences between them. That intensity creates an emotional fusion between them. They are hooked in to each other. The system gets tighter, like the stretched rubber bands.

Emotional fusion is what happens when we have difficulty separating self from the other. How the other is affects how self is, and vice versa. For example, when arguments between two people escalate, each is reacting to how the other expresses self as much as to what is said. We say things like, "Her angry face makes me feel ..." There is the sense that how the other is "makes us" be a certain way, or do, feel, or say certain things.

We all experience this fusion to a greater or lesser extent in our relationships. No one is free of it entirely. But the more it can be reduced, the better we will be able to relate to each other in our differences.

Fusion is not all negative. Many of our expressions of loving and caring result from the way words and signals coming from the other stimulate similar feelings in us. This is part of the "falling in love" experience; however, that does not automatically make these feelings valid expressions of the other person's true intent. Willoughby, in *Sense and Sensibility*, knows how to use

34

this experience in his insincere seduction of Marianne Dashwood. As we might say today, "She falls for his line" because of her fusion with him. Her thinking and her feeling are significantly tied into him and his loving expressions toward her. So when he jilts her, she is as devastated as she had been exultant when she was sure of his love for her. Her sense of identity is fused with who she perceived him to be.

Fusion can get in the way of our being able to see objectively what is going on in a relationship. Being able to get more sense of emotional separateness (not distance) from the other, in our thinking and feeling, will help us more accurately understand what is happening in a relationship and how to be within it. It can lead us to a greater sense of the true closeness and intimacy that can occur between two people.

When fusion goes on for a long time, symptoms may develop in the emotional system. There are four main types of symptoms that show up when people have difficulties in their emotional relationships. All of my counseling clients had one or more of these symptoms:

1. emotional distance in relationships;
2. open conflict in relationships;
3. physical, emotional, or social difficulties in one partner; or
4. projection of anxiety to a child (who will then have physical, emotional, or social problems).

When emotional intensity happens in your family, it affects different members in different ways and to different degrees, but all will be touched. Whatever affects one member of the system will have an impact in the rest of the system. **It will be like an electrical charge in the system: everyone will feel some degree of shock.**

Reactivity in the Emotional System

When one person's actions do not fit in with the wishes or expectations of others, the others may react to those actions. Then, out of their own sensitivity, the first person may react to that reaction, and on and on it will go, sometimes for years. One common pattern is that we try to correct each other or straighten each other out—like with my use of the word "hero": some people will want to correct my "inappropriate" use of the term. We try to get people to agree with us and to change. This can create a lot of drama, because we may argue openly (symptom 2), or just inwardly withdraw (symptom 1). Think of what Elizabeth Bennet (in *Pride and Prejudice*) goes through when Charlotte, Elizabeth's good friend, agrees to marry Mr. Collins. She is upset that Charlotte would marry a man whom Elizabeth considered a fool. She distances from Charlotte and almost stops being her friend.

Here is another simple example of an emotional system at work for those of you who are parents. Think of a time when one of your kids had a problem. Or if your kids are grown up, think of how you feel if one of your adult kids calls to tell you about some significant difficulty, such as a serious illness, the loss of a job, a divorce, or some other disturbing event that gets them upset.

They call you with their anxiety and upset. What happens to you? Immediately your own anxiety kicks in, and you can feel something churning in your gut. You may even keep thinking about it obsessively after the phone call. You may have many questions. You may immediately start blaming someone or diagnosing the situation. You may start thinking about solutions, or what you could do to help, or how to stop whatever is going on. **You are emotionally hooked into the problem.** You have caught the anxiety that is in the emotional system.

I am not saying that this process is "bad." It is the normal way more fused emotional systems work. Think about the disturbance in the Bennet family (in *Pride and Prejudice*) when young Lydia, at the age of fifteen, runs off with Wickham who is maybe twenty-eight. Even Darcy, who is not a family member, is affected by Lydia going off with Wickham. On a daily basis, growing up within our families of origin, and then getting married and creating our own families, we all live out this emotional drama.

Austen wrote about ordinary families and ordinary heroes, as we are ourselves. Sir Walter Scott, a contemporary of hers who wrote grand, heroic novels about larger-than-life figures, said this about Austen: "That young lady has a talent for describing the involvements and feelings and characters of ordinary life which is to me the most wonderful I ever met with. The big bow-wow strain I can do myself like any now going; but the exquisite touch, which renders ordinary commonplace things and characters interesting, from the truth of the description and sentiment, is denied to me." Scott wrote this in his diary in 1826 (Austen's death was in 1817). He had just read *Pride and Prejudice* for the third time.

If you had significant issues with your parents growing up, or with your siblings, many of those same emotional issues probably still exist for you as an adult. In addition, your family's perception of their issues with you can be just as active now as fifty years ago. A friend of mine was surprised recently when he was confronted by a sibling of his who was carrying a forty-year-old resentment. My friend had long forgotten the incident, and he was amazed at the vehemence of his brother's feelings. Luckily, he had the maturity to not react to the feelings and to explore with his brother what it was all about and how to understand it now. Their relationship improved significantly as a result.

Time and Distance Do Not Fool an Emotional System

Here is an example from my family (see my simplified family diagram below). I am Ron (with double box around my name). My mother Naomi is listed above me with her four husbands to the right of her. I did not know my father, Preston. Marriages two and three lasted only six months each. Mike, the fourth husband, is the one she stayed with until he died. He had been previously married and had three children in that marriage. The double backslash lines indicate divorce. Over on the left of the diagram, Tom is my cousin, born to Blanche and Alton. Blanche is Mom's older sister and my aunt. Wallace, their brother, is the middle child.

My simplified family diagram

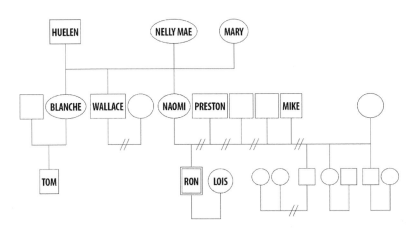

When my mother Naomi (who was in Los Angeles) was close to death and in the hospital, she had decided to not eat as a way to hasten her dying. I flew down from Vancouver to be with her. I also called my aunt Blanche in St. Louis (she was Mom's older sister by nine years) and told her what was happening, suggesting she might come out to say goodbye. She flew out the next day.

These two had not seen each other for many years—they had just occasional phone calls—but they were part of a long-term emotional system that had been through a great deal over the years. My then eighty-three-year-old aunt (a typical older sister in many ways) walked into Mom's hospital room, looked at the tray of uneaten food beside her bed, and her very first words to Mom were, "Sister, you're not eating your food." Her first words!

Blanche walked over to the bedside and started trying to feed Mom, who reluctantly took one small bite before closing her mouth and refusing any more food. My aunt said to her, "Sister, you're just as stubborn as you always were!" My mom immediately replied, weakly, "And you are just as bossy!" I found this hilarious, but of course I kept my laughter to myself. As children and young adults, they had fought around these kinds of issues, and repeated the same interactions over and over. It was automatic for them to have this exchange even at this stage of life. Throughout their adult lives with others, they both had strong reactions to people who were "stubborn" or "bossy."

This example shows something that often happens when we are hooked into these emotional system patterns: **we tend to send "you" messages**, as my mother and aunt both did when they each focused on the other's "problem." It also clearly demonstrated how quickly an emotional system can be activated after years of separation. It was as if an electromagnetic field switched on between them as soon as they were in the same room. Bowen once said, **"Time and distance do not fool an emotional system."**

If you were like my mom, and you started a new romantic relationship with someone who was an oldest sibling in their family, those automatic reactions to their "bossiness" would be activated. You would be sensitized to these patterns. That is what each of Mom's husbands ran into. According to her report, they all said to her, "You are too independent." If you were like her, you might never think, "Here I am replaying my old patterns with my older sister in this new relationship." You would be clear that you didn't like the bossiness, but you might not be aware of your part in the interaction. If the other person had some rebellious younger sibling, the two of you could really go at each other and not realize how your emotional systems, established long ago, were still running your life. For you both, it would be the same drama but with different players.

How Can We Change Our Systems?

Given these deeply engrained patterns of behavior, it is very difficult to create change in our relationships. We tend to continue with our old dramas, rather than learn new lines in a new play. Once a system has arrived at a homeostatic balance, like a mobile, it doesn't want to upset things further by creating change, because even good change automatically means instability. **The tendency of the larger system is to inhibit any move toward change.** We see how hard it is for Austen's characters, and we know how difficult it is for us as well.

But change is possible. I remember how scary it was to be more open and vulnerable with Lois about my inner life of feelings and thoughts. How would she respond? How judgmental would she be? Might she dislike me? So many feelings and questions can come up in the change process, and because it is new territory for us to explore, we don't know what we will find or what we will learn. This is why making changes in the homeostatic balance is anxiety-provoking—it is because of the fear of the unknown. We don't know what the new balance will be like, or even if there will be a balance. It could be a wreck.

All of this takes courage: the courage to be a different person. It helps, as a step in this direction, to be able to think about how our systems function so that we can get some sense of orientation to the larger picture of what is going on and how to change ourselves within it. The next few chapters will focus on gaining the necessary understanding. The last three chapters give some concrete suggestions for what to do to change our relationships, but putting those suggestions into action depends on using these earlier chapters to gain an adequate understanding of how emotional systems work. Without that understanding, the emotional system will always beat us into conforming to "the way we always do it." Our relationships will not improve, and we will think it is the other person's fault.

Questions to Ponder

1. Have you ever thought of yourself as belonging to a family emotional system? What might it mean to you to think of you and your family in this way?
2. Are there certain feelings you have long had about yourself? How do those feelings fit into your family system?
3. Do you tend to encounter the same feelings in your current adult relationships?
4. Of the four symptoms of emotional system difficulties listed earlier in this chapter, can you see any of them in your own life or your family life?
5. Give a shot at drawing your own family diagram. Does doing this stir anything up for you?

3

Watching Our Systems

in Action

You can observe a lot by watching.

Yogi Berra

In addition to the family emotional system, we belong to a number of other emotional systems (see diagram below). **This is the "country village" part of Austen's subject.** We interact with others in these various systems, and what happens in one can affect how we are in another. We all know how a bad day at the office can lead to a bad evening at home, and vice versa. We gain some of our identity from these other communities in the larger world and we bring some of that back into our family systems. Conversely, we also take some of our patterns from our family systems into these communities in a reciprocal way.

Some of our emotional systems

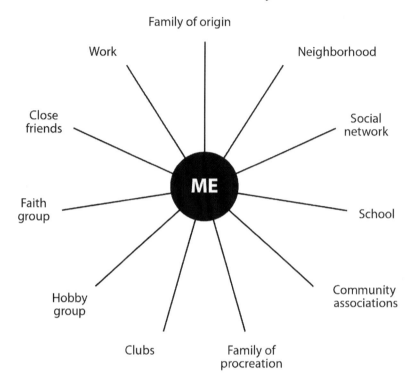

Not everyone in a system has the same level of impact or infringement on that system. They each have a different emotional impact, or influence in the emotional systems they are a part of, and they have differing levels of sensitivity to others in the system. A good example of this in Austen is how little direct impact Anne Elliot has with her father and sister in *Persuasion*. Early in chapter 1 we read: "Anne, with an elegance of mind and a sweetness of character, which must have placed her high with any people of real understanding, was nobody with either father or sister; her word had no weight . . . she was only Anne." She is only Anne. Her father's and sister's values and orientation about what is important in life is so different from hers that she doesn't count for them. At the same time, their visions of social grandeur have little impact on her. However, she has a great deal of influence in her own extra-family social system, as well as in her extended family system, and in roundabout ways, on her father and sister. They just don't recognize it.

Anne's mother dies when Anne is thirteen. In addition to being a personal loss, this shakes up her family system. Anne takes after her mother, who was a good and reasonable woman who could have kept the family on a realistic financial course. Anne transfers a lot of her parental feeling to her godmother, Lady Russell, a good friend of the family. That more fused emotional relationship gets her into some difficulty as a young woman because Lady Russell, who shares some of her father's values, persuades her to turn down Captain Wentworth's proposal for marriage.

Nine years later, when the opportunity with Captain Wentworth arises again, Anne has to learn how to address this relationship with Lady Russell in order to move ahead in her life with Wentworth. She has to find a way to reduce the level of fusion with Lady Russell without being critical of her or her influence. Without blaming her or attacking her, Anne takes responsibility for her own part in that relationship and for how she has been susceptible to Lady Russell's influence, or persuasion. This allows her to maintain a good relationship with Lady Russell as well as connect with the man she loves.

Gaining Perspective on Our Emotional Systems

One major benefit of Anne being more outside of her father's and sister's emotional system is that she has the clearest view of the effects of the family's profligate way of life. Because they cannot think realistically about their situation, they are coming to ruin unless they do something drastic. Lady Russell is one of the people enlisted to advise them. "But she had prejudices on the side of ancestry . . . which blinded her a little to the faults of those who possessed them. . . . She drew up plans of economy, she made exact calculations, and she did what no one else had thought of doing, she consulted Anne, who never seemed considered by the others."

With the help of a financial advisor, she and Anne are finally able to convince her father what he should do. It does not go exactly the way Anne wanted, but at least she has provided the necessary objectivity to help get the ball rolling.

The father and oldest daughter duo continue their error-filled ways even after they take the necessary action of renting out the estate and taking more modest accommodations in Bath, a resort spa town in southern England where Austen lived for a few years. They continue to live on their illusions of their importance, but Anne, content to go her own way without any interference from them, maintains a helpful outsider's perspective that helps somewhat to keep them from getting into too much trouble. She remains nonreactive to them and their values, and she does not angrily attack them or try to change them. She is also free to pursue connections with a whole other class of naval people that includes Captain Wentworth, and with one very important but poor person, Mrs. Smith, an old school classmate. Mrs. Smith provides some insider intelligence to help save her father and sister from some serious mistakes. These other social systems prove critical in Anne's life.

All emotional systems have their challenges and difficulties, but some function better than others do, even when they are faced with quite similar challenges and stresses on the system. If there is even one person in the system who is able to be more objective about the functioning of the system, and less reactive to how others are behaving, and who can personally act more maturely, that person will be a resource to the larger system. This is the case with Anne Elliot.

Another Austen character who possesses a similar family position as Anne, and who gradually develops the maturity of character to function well within her emotional system, is Fanny Price in *Mansfield Park* (see Appendix III for the family diagram). Fanny, who is a niece to Sir Thomas and comes from a very poor family, comes into his family as an outsider. Mrs. Norris, her aunt, suggests that Sir Thomas invite her into the family. The family treats her as an outsider for much of the book. Early on, she is unable to act effectively within that system, primarily because of her anxiety. In a masterful piece of writing, Austen shows us, in realistic terms, over the course of the novel, how Fanny slowly overcomes her anxiety and becomes, eventually, a more significant and valued member of the family.

Learning to "Think Systems"

It is automatic for us to think in individualistic terms. To learn what makes for good relationships, we have to look beyond the individual and learn to see people in context. What is it that gives them their sense of self and how they function in the world? We get our sense of self, first, in our families, and then in the other systems we are a part of. In *Persuasion*, Austen places Sir Walter Elliot and his oldest daughter Elizabeth in the context of a minor aristocracy. The book opens with him reading about his personal entry in the *Baronetage*: "Sir Walter Elliot . . . was a man who, for his own amusement, never took up any book but the *Baronetage*; there he found occupation for an idle hour, and consolation in a distressed one . . . there he could read his own history with an interest which never failed."

Their values around what is important in the world are superficial. Being a part of this aristocratic group is what gives Sir Walter his identity, but he treats it as if it were his personal accomplishment. They do not have the insight to understand that their way of life, the system they belonged to, is dying out, just like their personal finances are. They cannot see that newcomers on the stage of life, the emerging middle class, are becoming more influential. The group of naval officers that Anne falls in with are an example.

It does not come naturally to us to think in terms of systems. We were taught the individual model from day one. We learned that there are "good" children and "bad" children, and we were told which one we were. This way of thinking spread from the family to school to work and to various other activities. It is a lot easier to put individuals, like Sir Walter, under the microscope of evaluation than to think of the larger systems they are a part of. Austen's Anne could see the bigger picture and Sir Walter could not.

When we function out of the individual model, we blame individuals for their "bad" behavior. We become critical of them. Perhaps we even tell them how awful they are. We may try to straighten them out. This feeling-based reactivity is a sign of our fusion with the other person. We are in and of the system. Anne in *Persuasion* is mostly outside the system formed by her father and sister. She is more mature. She is not angry with them and does not attack them for their shallow values. She can see where they get their sense of self. She cares for them and tries to do right by them without judging them severely. If she was reactive to them, or tried to change them, she would be caught up in their emotional system.

As a therapist, I always looked at the family of the person I was working with to understand their "bad" behavior. I did this even with those who had little ongoing contact with their family of origin, because **lack of contact does not mean lack of influence**. Remember the meeting between my mom and my aunt after several years of not seeing each other. As my clients re-engaged with their family of origin and worked at understanding it better, they saw themselves as a part of that system. Rather than just blaming various members of the family, they took responsibility for their own functioning within that system. They focused only on changing self with them, not trying to change them. They also started doing a better job in their current adult relationships since they could see them in context as well.

Changing Our Feelings

Our feelings run all of us to some extent. Our inner, subjective feelings occur within specific outer, more objective contexts and relationships. The feelings connect to these contexts and have significance within them. Being a part of the aristocracy caused Sir Walter to feel disdainful of those who were not. Our feelings cause us to be reactive with important people in our lives, but how can we break that pattern? A key part of doing this is learning to think in terms of systems rather than individuals.

If you have a parent or a sibling, for example, whom you have been quite reactive to (for example, you have distanced from them, fought with them, or tried to change them), how could you behave differently with them? You could become curious about them, be interested in them, and learn more about how they got to be "that way." What is important to them? If you have your own diagnosis of them, then you are missing the point. What is their perspective on the issue? When we do this, we reduce our emotional reactivity to them and step out of the fusion with them. We are taking greater responsibility for our own way of being with them (that is, being less reactive and more proactive). In Bowen theory, we call this "taking a research stance."

It is normal for us to have feelings within our various important relationships. Some of these feelings are wonderful and bring us closer to the people we want to be together with. But when we are reactive to them and start wanting to change them, or resisting their efforts to change us, we are caught up in the fusion and fail to see the larger system.

Our subjective individual feelings always have an emotional system context, and whatever feelings we are having at any particular moment reflect our position in the system. **A change in the objective position of a person in the system will lead to different subjective feelings.** Having a research stance is one way we can do this. With changed feelings, we can act more maturely.

If Anne had wanted to be a part of her father's and sister's world, then she would have felt resentful and angry with them for excluding her. She would have thought, "They should include me more." Not having expectations of how others should be is one way to get outside the emotional system and to relate to others in a more positive way. This is another aspect of the research stance: it helps us let go of how others "should be" with us and to focus on how we want to be with them.

Observing Our Family Emotional System

Bowen family systems theory gives us a way to understand relationships. As we observe the system, the theory helps us organize the information we gain and focus on helpful responses. One of the primary skills that I helped clients develop was being better observers of the various emotional systems they were a part of, and of their own reactions within those systems, and what they typically did with their reactions. Thinking about their own functioning in the system and changing their part, rather than focusing on changing others was a source of great learning for them. Austen's heroes do the same thing as they work at improving their relationships with others.

Elinor, in *Sense and Sensibility*, is one of the best examples in Austen. As she learns more about Edward's secret engagement to Lucy and works at developing a bigger picture of what is going on, she is able to reduce her reactivity and relate to all involved in a more balanced way. Had she not been able to do this, the whole situation might have blown up, leaving everyone feeling damaged and no one happy. It was her maturity in being able to handle this that brought about the positive changes that we all rooted for.

When we find a potential partner, someone we love and want to be with, it is ideal if we can gain some sense of that person's family and how they behave within their family. In Jane Austen's time, among the gentry class, people would stay at each other's country estates for weeks or even months at a time. This gave them plenty of time to observe the functioning of the families that they might be marrying into.

We can do this work on our own if we are motivated to do it. We don't have to be in therapy. In part, the work starts with **becoming observers of the family emotional process rather than being interpreters of motivations and assigning blame.** Most of Jane Austen's heroes are excellent observers of what is there in front of them. When they fail to do so is when they get in trouble. Our fantasies can so influence our ability to see that we can't observe reality. Emma Woodhouse, in *Emma*, is a great example of this. She believes her imagination more than what is right in front of her. She totally misses that Mr. Elton is pursuing her and later thinks Frank Churchill must be in love with her.

Many people who are in love fail to see all of what is going on. When we are in love, we tend to see what we want to see, or we narrowly focus only on certain attractive qualities and ignore other qualities. This is the case with Marianne Dashwood in *Sense and Sensibility*. She so much wants Willoughby to be a certain way that she misses what is actually true about him. She cannot see how he is making himself into what she wants for his own ends. The same thing may be true when we decide not to like somebody. Elizabeth Bennet and Darcy, in *Pride and Prejudice*, show how our subjective feelings can warp our view of reality and we can build a case against another person that is not warranted by the facts.

In Bowen theory, we focus on the "functional facts" of a relationship system. **This means, who moves when, how or in what way; what is the response of others; and what is the response to the response?** We don't speculate about people's inner experiences, like their motivations; instead the focus is on actions. It does not help to ask "why" questions ("Why did you do that?") because the answers are usually speculative and can be unending. Think of the child who keeps asking "Why?" in response to every answer given. This is what many people do in their relationships, and spending time on this question does not change anything. We are often experts on what we think motivates other people and diagnosing what we think their problems are. That won't change things. That is the individual model at work. When we do this, we leave ourselves out of the equation, and we don't see our part in it all. Both Elizabeth and Darcy grew as people when they included themselves in the bigger picture. They were starting to think in terms of systems.

Becoming an observer of the emotional system is like sitting at the top of the football stadium: we see the bigger picture. It is better than being down on the sidelines, or even out on the field, where we have a more limited view. Football coaches have some of their coaching staff sitting up in the skybox level. They are observing the larger whole of the game and can call down to the head coach on the field and say, "Here is what is going on . . ." The coaches need that larger view of the action on the field. To see the whole system at work rather than just the individual players is essential to understanding the game and being better at it. When we are in love, it is hard to gain that perspective, but it is essential to achieving good relationships.

Marianne in *Sense and Sensibility* takes a long time before she can gain this perspective and let go of her fantasies about Willoughby and their relationship. She gets there eventually. Her sister Elinor does an incredible job of being able to see the bigger picture as her love interest Edward distances from her and she learns of his secret engagement to Lucy. This ability keeps her from acting in hasty and inappropriate ways and allows her to unite with Edward eventually. Austen shows us the kind of maturity that Elinor needs to make this happen.

As we learn to observe the functioning of the emotional system, and we see how we are a part of the process, we can begin to think more clearly about how we are functioning in it. Then we can think about how we would like to act. This is what I did in connecting with my own family of origin.

I used to stew resentfully on the fact that my mother did not ask me questions about my life. I know that many people would find this a blessed relief, but with me there were almost no questions at all, even while I was growing up. She appeared to show very little interest in my life and accomplishments. It took me some time to get to where I could be more neutral, and not angry, about this. Once I began this work, during an easy conversation, I was finally able to comment on this with her and talk about it calmly. I said to her, "Mom, I always knew you loved me, but I didn't think you were interested in me." She said, "Why would you say that? I have always been interested in your life." I said, "Well, you never ask me any questions." She kind of symbolically slapped her forehead and told me this behavior stemmed out of her own family experience. Once she explained the larger family context, I understood that it didn't have to do with me, and that it wasn't just her own individual personality quirk.

Her older sister and brother were old enough to remember their mother before she died. They knew and loved her. They resented their stepmother, Mary, when she came into their lives three years later. Their father did not know how to make this transition in the family go smoothly and great distance developed between the two of them and her. They could not develop a bigger picture and were just reactive to her, as she was to them. She became, for them, the "wicked stepmother." The emotional process took over between them all, and no one was able to be different within it.

My mom was only three years old when Mary came into her life. Mary became "Mom" for her. All three siblings described her as a jealous and possessive woman who kept my mom close to her while growing up, and she would not let my mom get close to her father. She was jealous of Mom's father's loving feeling for Mom. Mom gave me many examples of how Mary kept them apart. The issue of not asking questions came out of this. Even when my mom was a young adult, her stepmother questioned her about everything: Where have you been? How did you get there? Who were you with? What did you do? And so forth. The fusion was so strong and intrusive that Mom had little sense that she could be her own person. This resulted in her assertive individuality later as an adult, and she also said to herself, **"I will never do that to my child!"**

When the issue of Mom's behavior was put into that context, my perception of her way of being with me totally changed. As a result, I gained a new position in the system, and the feelings of resentment melted away. I started to think about what kind of love it must have taken for her to live up to her commitment even when I was so clearly keeping her out of my life. Because I thought she wasn't interested, I did not volunteer things with her. I did not see my mom as a resource for issues in my life and talk with her about them, because of this. This applied to so many aspects of our life together.

The fusion with her and her mom transferred into her relationship with me, and we carried it on through our distance from each other, equally fused but in a different way. Early in my life, I actually was suspicious of people who asked me questions. I thought, What do they want? What are they up to? This was the case when I married Lois. I wanted people to be interested in me, but I thought there must be some other agenda if they asked about me. This obviously created a double bind for others.

Jane Austen on Changing Self in the System

A perfect example of someone gaining a wider perspective and changing their behavior as a result is in *Pride and Prejudice* when Elizabeth begins to think through her stance toward Darcy. Originally, she diagnoses him and focuses on how rude, proud, and arrogant she thinks he is. After a major negative encounter with him (when he makes his first incredibly bad proposal), and then receiving his letter of explanation, which challenges the way she has been observing relationships with him and with Wickham, and gradually seeing how wrong and blind she had been, she gets in touch with the bigger picture. She sees how she has been moving in the system and how she has missed important facts. She becomes more objective and steps outside her subjectivity. Once she sees herself anew within the emotional system, she is truly horrified with herself. She says, "I had never known myself." Her feelings begin to change.

As I understood better my mom's reasons for acting as she did, I decided that when I wanted her to know something about me, I would just tell her and not wait for her to ask. As it turned out, she loved knowing about my life. **I had been waiting for her to ask, and she was waiting for me to tell her.** Although I had been blaming her, I could now see that my distance had perpetuated the emotional process between us and given me my bad feelings and resentment. It was not just about her. I was a part of this fused emotional system that created the feelings in me. Those feelings stopped once I understood. As Elizabeth Bennet says, "I had never known myself": I had never seen my part in the emotional process.

If we want to improve our relationships, we have to learn to see the bigger picture. We have to put other people into a context that explains who they are and how they learned to function in that context, and then we have to include ourselves in the system. Like soap operas, our own lives are full of reactive patterns that can go on for years and years with essentially no change, unless someone decides to do it differently. That is where the courage to change comes in.

Jane Austen not only shows the dilemmas and problems of family life (and other difficult relationships)**, she also shows how her heroes think their way through the situations** and manage to change and function better as a result.

Questions to Ponder

1. Apart from your family, what other emotional systems are powerful in your life? What do they add to your own identity?

2. How do you function within your other emotional systems? Is your functioning the same as it is in your families of origin and procreation, or different? How do you understand that?

3. Were you a more important or less important member in your family of origin? What was that like for you? Were there advantages and disadvantages to this?

4. If you have begun to have a systemic perspective on your family, how do you describe it, and how do different members function within it?

5. If you have not yet developed that perspective, how could you move in that direction?

4

Anxiety Can Really Upset an Emotional System

Anxiety creates its own disaster.

Gregory Bateson

Imagine your fifteen-year-old daughter running away with a man who is almost twice her age. What would you experience as a parent? How about the rest of the family; how would they react? What would you each do? In *Pride and Prejudice*, this is what happens when the youngest daughter, Lydia, runs off with Wickham. She thinks Wickham wants to marry her, but that is not his intent.

With this event, the emotional system of the Bennets starts spinning wildly out of control. They are all full of anxiety. Anxiety underlies almost every problem we have in relationships. Whether it is blatantly and openly out there or hidden behind any number of other feelings, it is all about us getting anxious. **Anxiety is our reaction to any sense of threat, whether real or imagined.** For example, arguments, fear of our loved one leaving us, fear of not being loved, jealousy, or a teenage child running away all create that sense of threat to what we want.

Anxiety can really put our emotional systems into a spin and create havoc in relationships. Using the image of the mobile, anxiety is like a powerful wind that blows through it and upsets the balance. All relationship systems are subject to the forces of anxiety. Anxiety is an alarm mechanism that warns of an emotional threat. There are many potential triggers for eliciting it.

We all experience anxiety to some degree. We show our level of maturity both in how anxious we are generally, and in how we handle it when we are anxious. **All of Austen's heroes have times of anxiety, especially in relation to the people they love.** They each face the potential loss of that person. However, they each, in their own way, show us mature ways to deal with it. Each novel also has someone in the role of "the other woman." Those who are in that position are also anxious, and in each case, they show us the less-than-mature ways to handle their sense of threat.

When my college girlfriend June broke off the relationship with me (she had found someone else), her action threatened the trajectory of my whole life. In my fusion with her, she had been central to what I had imagined for my life. I didn't know what to do or even who I was without her. I was an emotional mess. I was so disoriented that I took a year off from graduate school to come to terms with the upset and think about my future.

We can imagine potential threats that may never really occur, but we can act as if they have or will. We call this conscious part of anxiety "worry" or "concern." For example, Mrs. Bennet worries about, or sees the potential threat of, her five daughters staying unmarried. She aims much of her activity in the story at trying to deal with this threat. This single-minded, anxious focus makes her appear to go over the top in her behavior, and also provides some of the humor of the story.

Anxiety is not just an individual phenomenon. **Anxiety is highly infectious.** It is the major driver of the emotional process in our families, and in other groups we are a part of. Wherever people are gathered, there will anxiety be also, in variable amounts, perhaps significantly at some point. Whole families can be involved as in chapter 46 of *Pride and Prejudice,* with Lydia running away with Wickham. Even Darcy is anxious although we don't find out about this until much later.

Anxiety causes all sorts of hormones to be dumped into our physical system. These create the famous fight-or-flight reaction to threat. This is the important positive side to anxiety. **Anxiety stimulates us to take action in dangerous situations.** These reactions, however, are for dealing with real attacks as in cave man days, like from cave bears or saber-toothed tigers, or attacks from neighboring tribes. These physical reactions are almost useless in many modern-day emotional challenges; often, acting on them only complicates our lives and relationships. When we react quickly rather than taking time to think about what is happening, we can make things worse. Our bosses may fire us if we tell them what we really think of them.

Jealous or jilted partners may act in ways that make things worse for them rather than better. The cave man part of me wanted to do something to win "my June" back to me, but if I had tried to do that, I probably would have made things worse. Instead, since I could do nothing about the loss, I fell into a depression. Much depression is an anxiety-based reaction to some kind of loss in our lives that we feel powerless to do anything about. Loss is a threat to our life as it has been.

Acting out of their anxiety, the Bennet family attempts to go after Lydia and take her back from Wickham. However, neither Mr. Gardiner, Lydia's uncle, nor Mr. Bennet are able to find her. As a result, the family becomes depressed. Darcy, on the other hand, knows something of Wickham's ways and knows where he might find him. He makes effective use of his anxious energy to save the day. Since Lydia will not leave Wickham, he makes Wickham marry her.

When there is an upset in our family or in an important relationship, and we can't get the outcome we want, we may just walk away and try to ignore the situation. We say, "I can't change anything here so I just have to get away." We distance. We want to find a way to calm down, and distance can help in the short run. We may take a holiday, or find some kind of distraction, and that may help us get some perspective and lead to some resolutions about how to be. Alternatively, less helpfully, we may medicate ourselves with drink, dope, or pills.

Acute and Chronic Anxiety

There are two kinds of anxiety: acute and chronic. **Acute anxiety is usually about threats related to real external events** like, for example, natural disasters such as earthquakes, fires, and floods. In this way, acute anxiety is like fear. Some specific event happens that inspires a sense of threat. We have an anxious feeling that is related to the fear of some kind of hurt and uncertainty as to what will happen. The anxiety is the sense of threat and the fear is of a specific threat. When the fire alarm goes off in your home or office, most of us feel some acute anxiety. Or we may feel physically threatened by another person, by someone who is angry enough that they want to hit us, or by a robber, or as a soldier in war, and so on. Certainly, the actual loss of a loved one who dies or leaves us makes us feel acute anxiety. The actual event of Lydia running away is about acute anxiety.

Acute anxiety is like wind blowing on a mobile. The mobile moves in response, but once the wind has stopped, the mobile can usually get back into balance as it gradually calms down. People are generally good at dealing with acute anxiety. As sad and scary as it is, for example, people who have lost their homes due to tornadoes, fires, or floods do, after some time, recover. The Bennet family does eventually recover and adjust to the new situation with Lydia and Wickham. We all survive in these situations, hopefully, individually and as a group because we have this anxious reaction and can use the energy it gives us to carry on with what needs to be done.

Chronic anxiety is about the imagined sense of threat. In our imagination, we can live in constant fear of a windstorm blowing through the mobile. Mrs. Bennet lives with the fear that her daughters will never marry. While the fear could be based in reality, she perceives the threat as being so serious that she lives in a somewhat unrealistic world, constantly vigilant for a possible suitor for one of her daughters. Even Lydia running away and marrying Wickham is a kind of a plus in her eyes: she says to herself, "Well, that's one taken care of." Elizabeth herself moves quickly into some chronic anxiety in fearing that with Lydia running off with Wickham, with this shameful thing happening in her family, Darcy will want nothing to do with her.

Here is a more contemporary example. A woman dies from a fatal illness and leaves her husband to cope with their three young children on his own. There is acute anxiety related to the actual loss of the wife and mother. There can be a degree of chronic anxiety on the father's part because he doubts his ability to cope with this new situation. This actually happened in my mother's family when their mother died. Their father (my grandfather) could not cope with raising three young children and running his farm. For three years, he turned his three children over to his parents until he remarried. That family never got fully back on track because the new wife quickly became the wicked stepmother. She became the focus of the anxiety in the family, and issues around her carried on for a long time. I inherited some of those issues, as I described in the last chapter. The anxiety carried on into how Mom parented me, and then that became a part of how I lived my life. **The effects of anxiety can be passed down through the generations.**

As I came to know my family's history, I found out how anxiety and the sense of threat in each of the members affected this family and me. It took a long time for their "family mobile" to recover and rebalance. The new homeostasis, once reestablished, was not a fully happy or healthy one.

Nearly all of Austen's novels begin with some sort of acute anxiety situation and then show how that plays out in the families, depending on their level of chronic anxiety. *Sense and Sensibility* starts with the death of Mr. Dashwood and the remaining family of wife and three daughters have very little income to live on. In addition, they have to move out of their family home. The Bennet family in *Pride and Prejudice* will eventually face the same situation in the future when Mr. Bennet dies. This threat is a real one for them. In *Persuasion,* a reduced family income forces that family to move out of their grand estate home.

Think about what it was like in *Emma* for Mr. Woodhouse and Emma as changes occur for them. First his wife (her mother) dies. Some new balance is set when Miss Taylor enters the family and becomes the family caregiver for both Mr. Woodhouse and his two daughters. He, especially, becomes highly dependent on her. Then his oldest daughter, Isabella, marries and moves away. Then when Miss Taylor herself marries Mr. Weston and moves away, there is more upset in the family. Mr. Woodhouse, in particular, has great difficulty coping and moans about her loss nonstop. The losses have piled up for him, and his chronic anxiety, expressed often as hypochondria or the inability to cope with even normal changes like a light snowstorm or the way his oatmeal is prepared, is a challenge for them all.

In each of these cases, **the real, acute anxiety is heightened by the level of imagined, chronic anxiety** involved. We all have some level of chronic anxiety; some of us more and some of us less. A person who has a higher level of chronic anxiety, for example, will have a bigger reaction to a partner being angry at them than will a person with a lower level. It can be the same expression of anger by the partner, but the reaction in the other will be determined by their level of chronic anxiety. A less chronically anxious person may say, "Okay, I hear you are angry. Tell me about it." A more chronically anxious person may think, "Oh no, she wants to leave me." Or, "He wants a divorce. I will be lost without him." Or any number of other scary scenarios.

The level of chronic anxiety will be a major factor in our ability to deal with the real situations in our life. We all have a certain amount of emotional immaturity and chronic anxiety, and we all have variable degrees of flexibility and adaptability to new circumstances. The higher the chronic anxiety, the more difficult it is for us to flex and adapt. Mr. Woodhouse could not comfortably adapt. We can begin to exaggerate the seriousness of events and develop fears for the future. Mr. Woodhouse acts as if his world has fallen apart since Miss Taylor left. This is part of the reason that Emma never considers getting married. She cannot think of putting her father through another one of these losses.

Chronic Anxiety Narrows Our Perspective

In Latin, the word for worry or distress (*angor*) shares the same root as the English "anger" and "anguish." It means "to narrow" or "choke." **We narrow our focus when anxious**—usually to the one thing we think is threatening us, and we may ignore many other related critical factors in a situation. Mrs. Bennet is so eager to get her daughters married that she misses the danger posed by Wickham. When we focus too narrowly on fixing the symptom, we will not deal well with the underlying issues that produced the symptom. Darcy focuses narrowly on hiding a shameful event in his own family involving Wickham, and fails to notice Wickham's threat to the Bennet family.

This is the kind of thing that happens to us when, for example, we get jealous. Jealous people are famous for not seeing the big picture, and this is how they undercut their own cause. Elinor Dashwood in *Sense and Sensibility* is an example of someone who handles her jealous feelings extremely well. She can see the bigger picture of how Edward got into this situation with Lucy, and even feels some sympathy for him. She does not focus narrowly on Lucy or want to hurt her, or express anger at Edward.

When we are chronically anxious, part of the difficulty is that we can easily lose perspective. You may remember the old pinball machines, where you scored points by getting the ball to hit as many possible obstacles as you could while keeping the ball in play. Sometimes it helped to give the whole machine a nudge to affect the path of the ball. However, if you pushed the machine too hard, it would register a "tilt" and then it would be game over. Different pinball machines had differing levels of sensitivity to being nudged or pushed. Some tilted easily and some could take a lot of pushing.

We are like that with our chronic anxiety. Some more emotionally mature family systems, and individuals within them, can take a lot of pushing and maintain their equilibrium, and some who are less mature can't take much pushing at all. They "tilt" easily, and things go haywire in their life as a result.

Chronic anxiety is not a good or bad thing. It just is. How much we have usually depends on the family we grew up in. We tend to catch our chronic anxiety from that family. We can imagine our personal level of chronic anxiety as existing on a scale of 0 to 10. Nobody is at 0 unless they are dead. A few of us live our lives at the less-anxious level of 2 or 3. People who are at the low end generally do well around whatever life presents them with. They are more emotionally mature. When bad things happen in their lives (causing acute anxiety), they have the emotional resources of flexibility and adaptability to deal with these events. Those people tend to make good decisions for their lives regardless of what they are up against.

Austen's more mature heroes, like Elinor in *Sense and Sensibility*, Elizabeth in *Pride and Prejudice*, and Anne in *Persuasion*, demonstrate these kind of abilities due to their lower level of chronic anxiety. This is what makes their lives go relatively well. When our level of chronic anxiety is low, we can focus better on essential skills for living a good life. Here are some results.

1. We develop values and principles that guide us in life and in our daily decision-making, and by which we actually live.
2. We don't spend a lot of time regretting past bad decisions or focus on blaming others for how our life has gone.
3. We develop the ability to think through our problems, see the bigger picture, identify the things we are dealing with, and develop reasonable, workable plans for action.
4. We are flexible if those plans don't work out and can adapt and change our plans.
5. We have the emotional skills for dealing with the variety of relationships and situations we are a part of in a competent and mature way.

Others of us have our levels of chronic anxiety set at, say, 6 or 7. It is a lot harder for us to live life with consistent equilibrium. Our relationship mobile is frequently unbalanced. We cannot consistently live by the skills listed above. Like Mr. Woodhouse, many things seem threatening or problematic for us. Life and the normal progression of challenging events is just harder for us. Things never seem to go well. Like Mr. Woodhouse, we need lots of support to make it in life.

People at the highest levels of chronic anxiety seem to go from one crisis to another. With levels like 8 or 9, they have great difficulty maintaining stable relationships. Many of these people end up on the street, or in prison, or in some sort of institution that will manage their lives for them.

For those of us in the middle range of chronic anxiety, there will be periods of calm and then of turbulence that will take us some time to recover from. If we have people in our lives who we can count on, it may be slightly better for us. More often, people in the upper ranges have relationships that are unstable and challenging. The relationships themselves can stimulate anxiety. Hermit-like, some people withdraw socially. Part of the problem is we count on our relationships to keep us calm, happy, and feeling secure, but that is usually asking too much of them. I wanted June to help me feel better about myself. This is part of how I was emotionally fused with her. If she loved me, then I was okay. Her loss unbalanced me; I was no longer okay. In terms of the mobile, things can easily start spinning wildly and get unbalanced, as there is anxiety in wanting the relationships with the others to help us feel safe emotionally.

When we depend on our relationships with others to help us feel okay in life, we are setting ourselves up for turmoil. It is good to have good relationships and to be able to enjoy them. When having them becomes the goal of our lives, or when being loved by someone is essential to our feelings about ourselves, and our sense of security, we are asking too much of our relationships. The relationships will not go well because we have unrealistic expectations of what they can do for us. Having good relationships depends on having realistic expectations for what they can do for us.

The Antidote for Chronic Anxiety

We do not have to be run by our chronic anxiety. It is possible for us to grow emotionally and thereby change how much anxiety runs our life. The antidote to chronic anxiety in Bowen theory is called differentiation of self. I will say more about this concept later in chapter 9. Differentiation involves being able, among other things, to not depend on relationships to calm us and make us feel okay. The better differentiated we are, the better our relationships will be. This is the major quality of Austen's heroes. Of course it is difficult not to depend on others for our sense of safety and calm. It is difficult not to be infected by the anxiety in the emotional system and not to add to it with our own, and yet to still actively relate to the other anxious members in the system. However, when we can do this, the general level of anxiety in the family will go down. Relationships will get better. **It is as if one part of a turbulent mobile can anchor in place and stay stable.** Then the other parts of the mobile will gradually calm down as well. Note that this does not mean distancing from others. We can all use distance as a way to calm down ourselves, but that is not differentiation, and it does not change things in the system.

Anxiety and Our Family of Origin

Generally, calmer and less anxious parents tend to produce calmer and less chronically anxious children. Conversely, children who grow up within a chronically anxious household tend to have a tougher time becoming competent adults themselves. Emotionally, they develop the higher level of chronic anxiety just by virtue of growing up in that less-stable and frequently chaotic environment. They will experience a higher sense of threat in life generally. For them, relationships will be more problematic.

It is in the nature of children to be attentive to and responsive to anxiety in the parents and to respond to that anxiety by becoming more anxious as well. As this pattern repeats over the years of growing up, it becomes part of the nature of the child. When that child becomes a parent, the pattern repeats with their children, and so on down through the generations. I watched my mother react to potentially upsetting situations with a significant level of calm, and I saw that she was able to get on with her life. I never consciously thought of this fact, but it became a part of who I am—for the most part.

This is true also in the animal world. Lois and I go ocean kayaking up in our part of the world, in British Columbia. We frequently come upon seals resting on rocks as we paddle by. When there are seal pups with their mothers on the rocks, we see the pups look at us and then look at the mother, wondering if there is a threat involved in our presence. The pup takes its cue from the mother. If the mother becomes agitated and quickly goes into the water to escape the threat, the pup follows. That pup quickly learns to avoid kayakers even though we are not a threat. They imagine us to be a threat. That is out of their chronic anxiety.

On the other hand, if the mother takes a look at us, sees that it is just more of those pesky kayakers who may disturb the serenity of life but are not a threat, and so lays her head back down to enjoy basking in the sun, so does the pup. All is well. If that pup is female, and grows up to have her own pups, she will most likely communicate a similar lower level of chronic anxiety when kayakers are around and not tend to imagine threat when it is not there. This helps explain the variety of reactions we get from seals, and the variety of reactions we get from people.

For humans, it may take rational thought to decide first, whether we are really threatened, and second, what would be the most effective thing to do about it if we are. **It is important to be able to distinguish real threats from imaginary threats**. However, we are not so good at making these distinctions and thinking clearly if we are chronically anxious. Elinor Dashwood in *Sense and Sensibility* is excellent at distinguishing real from imaginary threats as she deals with the threat that is Lucy Steele. She does not let her imagination take over and control her with chronic anxiety. Elinor stays close to Lucy, rather than reacting to her, attacking her, and distancing from her, and she stays focused on learning the facts of the situation. Knowing the facts helps ground her in reality.

Looking down through the generations of our own family, if we know anything about the families that resulted from the generations above, it can be somewhat easy to track which streams of our family had more chronic anxiety to deal with, and thus had more difficulties with life, and which had less.

I can see this in my own family. Bowen theory helps to explain much of the difference in different generational lines of my family (see my family diagram in chapter 2). My mother left my father when I was eight months old. I did not know him. Mom's second and third marriages (I was three and then fourteen) each only lasted six months. She married her fourth husband after I had left home and gone back east for graduate school. That was her longest marriage.

As I have said, my mother was the youngest of three children. The middle brother, my uncle Wallace, did not produce any children with just a brief marriage before he suicided with drugs and alcohol. The oldest sister, my aunt Blanche (nine years older than my mother and married long before my mother was), gave birth to a son (my cousin Tom) eight years after I was born. They desperately wanted him.

Life was significantly different for Tom, an only child with both parents, than for me, an only child living just with my mother. His parents had a much higher level of chronic anxiety. Like most oldest children, my aunt had many competencies, and if she had been born in a different age, she would have done very well in a career. But as a mother and along with her husband, they focused their anxieties on their son and were very protective; they worried about a lot of things for him. This significantly hindered his individual development. They were what is called "child-focused" parents. Tom's parents lived out a more anxious version of what they thought responsible parents should do. They were involved in most aspects of his life as he grew up, and he rarely made independent decisions. If he did, he usually could not follow through on them. As a result, he never got his life launched from home. He died at age forty-seven from alcohol and drugs, living at home, never having married.

On the other hand, being parented by my mother, the younger sister, was a different experience. She had not inherited a high level of chronic anxiety like her older sister. She was a laid-back and easygoing person. As a parent, she was concerned for my safety in a general way, and she loved me, but she left most decisions about how I would live my life to me. She really did see my life as my responsibility. She didn't want to interfere with that. In part, this was due to her experience with her stepmother.

In the seventh grade, in Los Angeles, I started getting jobs to earn money (she didn't have much to spare). I did this independently, without consulting her, and she asked practically nothing about my jobs. From that point on I was out and about in the world a lot on my own, and she was comfortable with that. She showed little interest in my schooling. She never attended a teacher's conference about me. She never asked whether I would go to college or not, and she was surprised when I, again without input from her, decided I was going to. She was further surprised when I decided to go to graduate school. She never once asked what I was going to do when I grew up, or how I was going to support myself in the decisions I made for my life. She just assumed I would figure these things out for myself and that it was not her job to live my life for me.

Unlike my cousin, I had relatively little chronic anxiety communicated to me from my mother. Mother mostly just looked after living her life in a responsible way, and she did most of that pretty well, except for the type of men she kept picking as husbands. Lucky for me, that was where her chronic anxiety focused. I learned to be responsible, mostly, and make relatively good decisions in life by watching her. She never verbally taught me "lessons" about life. **She taught by example.** She definitely had episodes of acute anxiety in her life, mostly involving men, but she just moved on and did not become overwrought by this.

In general, in spite of her marital issues, my mother felt a lot safer in the world than did my aunt and uncle. Her level of threat was much lower. When her marriages did not work out as she wished, she just walked away, divorced the men, and did not seek anything from them, like alimony or child support.

My aunt Blanche developed some of her chronic anxiety in an understandable way. She was old enough to remember the death of her beloved mother and the family chaos that followed. Her father, my grandfather, was not that competent at dealing with the family of three children, and Blanche, like many oldest daughters in these situations, took over, even when they lived with the paternal grandparents, who were also somewhat anxious people. She had to become the boss and developed enough chronic anxiety to see threats everywhere. It is no wonder she became such a protective and dominant parent. For her, life continued to be a precarious experience, and she had to be alert and protective of her son.

He grew dependent on that and never learned to be fully responsible for himself.

Questions to Ponder

1. Which of Austen's heroes do you think are most anxious and which are least anxious?
2. How has your anxiety been helpful to you?
3. In your own family of origin, how have you seen anxiety expressed? Were there periods of turmoil and upset? If so, what was the threat? Who has tended to be most susceptible to chronic anxiety?
4. What level would you put your own level of chronic anxiety at?
5. How has that affected your life?
6. What has been your most effective way of dealing with your anxiety?

5

Must We Bless
the Ties That Bind?

Let him who cannot be alone beware of community. . . . Let him who is not in community beware of being alone.

Dietrich Bonhoeffer

In *Sense and Sensibility*, Marianne says "I could not be happy with a man whose taste did not in every point coincide with my own. He must enter into all my feelings; the same books, the same music must charm us both."

Marianne claims to be very much her own person: an individualist in her thinking and feeling, unlike other people. Yet for her life partner, she wants someone who is exactly like her. That person must share with her the same outlook on life in every way.

There are two powerful forces in our lives. They give drama and vitality to our relationships. Austen describes them in all of her novels. They are the life forces for togetherness and for individuality. They are as basic to our lives as gravity. They are unseen, but their effect is always observable. These forces drive our emotional system. They exist within all of us. It is not too much to say that how well we manage them determines the quality of our relationships.

Togetherness and Individuality

One goal for happy relationships is to balance these forces. Although at various points in life, there may be good reasons to emphasize one over the other for a period, the goal is not to go too far in one direction or the other for any length of time.

Animals vary between species and within species in how much togetherness and individuality they display. Think of herd animals, or schools of fish, or some flocks of birds—they stay close together. They live their lives within large groups, acting at times as if they were one entity with one mind, like when you see a school of fish or a flock of birds all turn in the same direction at the same time.

Even then, from time to time in these species, we do see individual animals going their own way. You occasionally see a cow standing alone out in the field, away from the herd. One cartoon shows a lone cow in a field, with the herd way off in the background. A cowboy wants to bring the cow back to the herd, and the cow is saying, "Okay, okay, I'm coming. I just wanted some 'me' time."

In Bowen terms, it had abandoned the togetherness for some individuality.

Individual animals in some species are loners. They have very little to do with others of their own species except for times of mating. Only at those times are they more togetherness oriented. For example, unlike other great apes, the orangutans are like this—loners most of the time except for mating. Some of the big cat species are like this, but not all.

The Life Force for Togetherness

Much of the joy in life is about being together with others. Falling in love is a huge togetherness experience. For many people, it is an ecstatic one. Austen's novels reflect this kind of joy as things work out for her heroes at the end of the story. Of course, the sexual relationship can be one of our most intense and rewarding togetherness experiences. The birth of children and the creation of a new family is also a major togetherness goal.

The togetherness force is not just about our love relationships. **The human is one of the most social species on earth.** We tend to hang out with each other, for a variety of reasons, in both large and small groups. Sometimes, even in very large groups, we appear to be acting with a single mind. Think of the fans at a sporting event, cheering for their team. When the team scores, they erupt in joyful screaming together. Together, the fans can become ecstatic when their team is winning and despondent when it is losing. Or there might be a moment in church when the congregation or the choir is doing a particularly good job of singing a hymn. At a political rally, supporters yell their approval when they like something the politician has said. When an orchestra is playing well together, the musicians are as one, even though the individual instruments and the people playing them are so different. In business, the boss talks about the importance of employees being "team players."

There would be no human communities without the togetherness force. This force inspires people to perform heroic acts to support the group effort. This is often clearest in warfare, but there are many other examples. Both fear and courage can be contagious within the sphere of the togetherness force, producing mob hysteria or solidarity. When we are faced with a difficult challenge, such as a natural disaster, in our community, when we are threatened as a community or a society, we often decide to act as one body, "pulling together" to accomplish some goal.

At those times, we are susceptible also to a kind of "groupthink." Leaders tell us to go along with whatever is the party line. Especially **when we feel anxious, we can be very "togetherness" focused**. A contemporary example of this on a large scale is that in almost every country in the world, a certain portion of the population takes a strong anti-immigrant stance. There are usually two chronic anxiety-based fears involved here: first, that *they* are a dangerous threat; and second, that *they* are not like us and *they* will threaten our culture, or our way of doing things. This line of thinking holds that being together means all of us should be united and the same. Who is included in the term "we" is an aspect of the togetherness force. Some people are more inclusive than others are.

The Life Force for Individuality

When under the influence of the individuality force, we celebrate our uniqueness or our differences from others. Individual family members claim not to be like others in the family. You can have an art class (in which you are together) where everyone paints the same figure or the same scene, and yet each person's painting is different from the others. Each painting will be a unique expression of the person's way of seeing the world. That is part of what we like about art—the individual interpretation of what is being depicted.

We humans delight often in developing our own unique selves, to be our own person, doing what makes sense to us individually. At times, we wish to follow our own compass rather than the group compass. Individuality is what drives a child throughout the growing-up process to become unique based on their own thinking, beliefs, and wishes. It leads us to start having different thoughts and behaviors from our parents and our siblings, and eventually to leave the family and go out into the world on our own, to be our own person. Our individuality leads us to loosen the ties that bind.

Every great thinker, inventor, or explorer has had a strong dose of individuality. They may have had to go against the groupthink mentality of their colleagues or community and maintain their own unique directions in spite of others laughing at them. This has happened often in scientific communities when some researcher goes against the conventional thinking of other scientists. The psychoanalytic community of his day ridiculed Dr. Bowen (back in the 1960s and 1970s) because they did not agree with working with families rather than individuals. Now, most of his ideas are mainstream in the world of family psychotherapy.

Fusion and Individuality

Both individuality and togetherness can be subject to anxiety and emotional fusion. People like Marianne Dashwood in *Sense and Sensibility* may emphasize how they are different from others, saying that they are their "own person," out of fear of being lumped in with others that they disapprove of. Marianne attempts to base her identity on what she considers to be her uniqueness, but this is a reaction to others. She fears being thought conventional like others, and she goes to an extreme to show this. In doing this, it strains her relationship with others. She is frequently critical and rude toward them. Paradoxically, she has trouble accepting how others are different from her. Therefore, she needs a life partner who is just like her. All of this is basically an expression of her fusion with others. It is not true individuality.

Togetherness can also be an expression of emotional fusion, and this is where things can get most sticky in relationships. Bowen once called fusion "the undifferentiated family ego mass." It is a graphic term. **Emotional fusion occurs when it is hard to separate your own self from the other person.** My fusion with June was very powerful. That is why it felt like I lost my self when she broke up with me. My sense of self—of being an okay and acceptable person in the world—depended on her being in my life.

Anxious groups of people will promote fused togetherness. The higher the level of anxiety in any group of people, the more intense is the focus on unity as total agreement. When the togetherness force comes to the fore in anxious times, individuals will be strongly encouraged to suppress their own thoughts, beliefs, and principles in the fusion. Listen for how often you hear the word "together" from politicians. Ask yourself, "What is being asked of me? Do I agree? What will I have to give up in order to be together?"

It is not only leaders who push togetherness. As followers, we like being a part of a group that feels important to us. We like to be part of a cause we can believe in, along with others. When we face some major challenge or threat, we feel personally stronger and more competent as part of a group. We believe that **together, we can deal with the crisis and win the battle**. People who are fervent in their political beliefs may share this feeling. In times of war, there is a cohesiveness and willingness to accept orders, to subvert the self's wants to those of the commanders and to those of the cause.

There is a tendency to revile people who reject our group. Some people see conscientious objectors as "traitors." In the Vietnam War, however, and each of the wars since, there has been much less of a consensus about the war effort, and we have seen a widespread rebellion against the various wars. However, the dissenters have a togetherness force of their own, and they insist equally on unity for those on their side. Those who are pro-war and those who are anti-war each have their own fused togetherness-focused communities that they belong to. Within the two groups, it is also true that individual members are reluctant to say everything they truly believe, just in order to continue to be a part of their group. **We sometimes go against what we really believe just to be a part of the group.**

It can be the same in the two-person relationship of courtship when we are trying to win over someone we love. We can bend ourselves out of shape, not say everything we really believe or want in life, and try to fit in with the expectations of the desired other to win the acceptance and love of the one we are pursuing.

Charlotte Lucas in *Pride and Prejudice* does not act on her basic disdain of Mr. Collins; instead, she accepts his proposal for marriage in order not to become a poor spinster. When Elizabeth visits her, she finds that Charlotte has found a way to exist as an individual within that marriage, creating her own space within the house. Lucy Steele in *Sense and Sensibility* hides who she really is and wants to fit in with whomever she values as important to be connected with. Caroline Bingley in *Pride and Prejudice* keeps trying to convince Darcy that she thinks and feels just the way he does. Henry Crawford in *Mansfield Park* is nearly successful at making himself look as if he has changed and is an upstanding, moral man that Fanny might value.

My cousin Tom's side of the family was very togetherness focused, and there was less space for individuality. His parents expected him to think about life and its challenges the way they did. Even though he rebelled against his family's view, **his rebellion was still a sign of his fusion with them**, and he could not escape. This is often true of rebels. They have to stay connected to the family, or whatever group is involved, to play out their rebel role. He could not bless the ties he felt with his family. Several times, he said to me, "I wish your mother was my mother. You are so lucky."

On my side of the family, individuality was not only allowed but encouraged. Mother did it simply by staying out of the way, as I made my own way through life. She cared for me and loved me, but she did not expect that I should do with my life what she wanted. Mom never preached individuality, but she lived it herself. Each of her husbands complained that she was "too independent." She would not have chosen my life for herself, but she flexed and adjusted to the kind of life I developed and maintained love for me through it all. Our ties to each other were quite loose, but it still took me some time as an adult to "bless" them.

How to Balance the Two Life Forces in Your Relationships

In all of our close relationships, we have to find a balance between the two forces of togetherness and individuality. The more differentiated and less fused we are, the more we can do this. The more fused we are, the more often the forces appear to be in opposition to each other. Plenty of partners have the experience where one wants to do something "together" and the other wants to do "their own thing." Other couples do everything together and have practically no individual time, and others are just the reverse, hardly ever spending time together.

Two people may fall in love with each other believing that they are much the same, enjoy the same things, and share similar values, as the romantic Marianne Dashwood wants in a partner. Not long after getting married, however, they begin to discover their differences. They say things like, "I didn't know you thought that," or wanted that, or did that. They have the challenge of learning how to deal with their differences.

Jane Austen recognized this quite specifically, stating it in her uniquely ironic way in chapter 6 of *Pride and Prejudice*:

"Happiness in marriage is entirely a matter of chance. If the dispositions of the parties are ever so well known to each other or ever so similar beforehand, it does not advance their felicity in the least. They always continue to grow sufficiently unlike afterwards to have their share of vexation; and it is better to know as little as possible of the defects of the person with whom you are to pass your life."

In fact, this is a sharp observation. In the togetherness of marriage, **one or both partners can get anxious about too much closeness as sameness**. They can start feeling that they are losing self in the togetherness and become anxious. One or both will work at emphasizing difference as a way to maintain a sense of self, or individuality. We have to find ways to exist as individuals within our relationships and not simply become appendages of our partner, unlike Lady Bertram in

Mansfield Park. When we lose self, we can easily become depressed or, like her, have little ambition in life.

There is the romantic ideal that people in love should not experience much difference—they should be walking hand in hand into the sunset, on some beautiful beach, with no strife between them. Marianne Dashwood in *Sense and Sensibility* believes this. In chapters 10 and 31 there are passages where she rhapsodizes over how much she and Willoughby are the same. But her fusion-oriented romantic ideal is an illusion. In *Emma*, when Mr. Woodhouse complains that people are not more like him, Emma replies, "That is the case with us all, papa. One half of the world cannot understand the pleasures of the other." **The big challenge in all human relationships is keeping contact or closeness with each other in spite of our individual differences from each other.**

Of course, not all differences are problematic. Some differences we have can be quite acceptable to us and even entertaining. We can enjoy them, and we can as we say "celebrate" them. I love Lois's sense of humor. I enjoy it most when my anxiety is low. However, when it is high, and if it is aimed at me, then her humor starts to sound sarcastic or critical of me.

Emotionally, many of us wish that in our close relationships, in our marital and family life and our various communities, we could be like an orchestra where all of the members play their own individual instruments but play well together and produce beautiful music. However, to do this requires a musical score that everyone agrees to and a willingness to be led by the conductor. In marriages, family, and community life, we don't have such scripts. Of course, there are some dictatorial partners who enforce conformity on their partners and family members, even with violence, but this is not true unity.

We each try to create our own beautiful music of a relationship, and we vary in our ability to do this. **Each marriage and family is a creative act, and there is no one formula that fits all of them.** We are all different in this way. We all have to learn how to balance the two life forces in our relationships in our own way. The better differentiated we are, the better we can do it and with fewer problems. In more problematic relationships, one or both partners tend to emphasize the extremes and show little ability to work out their own comfortable patterns.

Emotional Fusion and Togetherness

Fusion is the opposite of differentiation. The togetherness force, especially when we are anxious, reinforces our emotional fusion and makes us feel that we should be the same in our approach to living a satisfying life. Rebelling against that idea, like Marianne Dashwood, is also about our fusion; it is not differentiation. When we got married, I really wanted Lois to enjoy downhill skiing with me. For a couple of years she tried to fit in with my wishes but kept finding that she just didn't enjoy it that much. I desperately wanted to ski with her, together, but she only enjoyed cross-country skiing, which I found too tame. Finally, she declared that she was done with downhill skiing. I felt abandoned, and she also felt abandoned that I didn't want to cross-country ski.

So this process can go both ways; both partners can push for sameness but around different issues, and they will get the same reaction from the other. Eventually Lois and I each accepted that what the other enjoyed was different and did not feel impelled to do what the other wanted. It was okay to be different and to go our separate ways in snow sports and other things.

We often think that closeness means sameness. In all of our relationships, with marriage being a prime example, we are trying to find a balance between being a self, being our own person, and being together and connected with others. On the other hand, we all prize our individuality. The less fused and more differentiated we are, the more accepting we can be of the other's individuality.

Austen and the Life Forces

The interplay of the two life forces creates much of the drama in Austen's novels. A good example is in *Mansfield Park* around chapter 32, when Sir Thomas is trying to convince Fanny to marry Henry Crawford. In his fused togetherness stance, Sir Thomas, along with other members of the family, insists that Fanny must agree with him and do as he wishes, which means marrying Henry. Sir Thomas thinks he is being responsible in pushing this marriage. He reacts to Fanny's display of individuality, when she says no to him, by calling her selfish and ungrateful. Ultimately, Fanny's individuality becomes an important force for the whole Bertram family. It actually helps them be more together in a more mature way, and they learn that her insights about the Crawfords were more accurate than theirs were.

Questions to Ponder

1. Can you see how the life forces of togetherness and individuality have played out in your life?
2. Have you pushed for more of one over the other in your relationships? At different times in life? How has that worked out for you?
3. When has fused togetherness become an issue for you?
4. When has your individuality been important to you in your relationships? How have you dealt with it, and how has that worked out for you?
5. Do you currently have a good balance of togetherness and individuality in your life with others?

6

Closeness and Distance in Relationships

I can't be alone, but I can't be too close.
Dorrie in *Stardust Memories*

In Genesis, it says that it is not good for man to be alone, but sometimes it is a great relief.
John Barrymore

Elizabeth Bennet says, "the far and the near must be relative." In chapter 32 of *Pride and Prejudice*, there is a rare encounter where Darcy and Elizabeth are together without anyone else present. They discuss several subjects, including how comfortable it is apparently for Charlotte Lucas (who has married Mr. Collins) to live some distance from her family home. Darcy, in a roundabout way, is also probing Elizabeth's willingness to live some distance from her family. His estate of Pemberley, in the Peak District, is a significant distance from Elizabeth's home. Elizabeth thinks he is talking about her sister marrying Bingley, and she does not want to make distance an issue. She says, "I do not mean to say that a woman may not be settled too near her family. The far and near must be relative, and depend on many varying circumstances."

As Elizabeth continues in this vein, "Mr. Darcy drew his chair a little towards her. . . . Elizabeth looked surprised. The gentleman experienced some change of feeling; he drew back his chair, took a newspaper from the table, and, glancing over it, said, in a colder voice: 'Are you pleased with Kent?'"

On the surface, the couple are discussing geographical closeness and distance, but their conversation is about much more at the same time. Misreading some of her signals, Darcy comes physically closer to Elizabeth. Her surprise about this causes him to back off. Notice the importance of nonverbal signals in this little dance. After he has left, as Charlotte and Elizabeth discuss the meaning of his visits, Charlotte raises with Elizabeth the possibility that Darcy is in love with her. Elizabeth did not find this likely, and yet she is mystified by how much he is visiting them, coming close.

The theme of closeness and distance between people runs throughout Austen's novels. At times, she shows it as actual physical movement, as in the passage we just saw. Austen often uses dancing as a metaphor for marriage; it captures the way people start together, separate, and then come back together. Henry

Tilney in *Northanger Abbey* specifically uses this image comparing dancing and marriage when he says, "I consider a country-dance as an emblem of marriage."

Emotional Closeness

In our relationships, **we expect some degree of emotional closeness**. People often think they are not close because they don't agree on some topics. Darcy pulls away when he thinks that Elizabeth is not on the same wavelength as he is. With her surprise at his move, she does not communicate a receptive response. Many couples have taboo topics, on a whole range of subjects that they cannot or will not discuss with each other. They have agreed, overtly or covertly, that they just "will not go there." This creates an uncomfortable distance between them.

Our relationships tend to cycle between times of closeness and of distance. It is normal to need some degree of closeness with others, and some degree of separateness or being alone and away from others. This is a part of the togetherness–individuality continuum in our lives. **Anxiety can impel us in either direction, either toward or away from others**, depending on who is involved, what is happening around us, our particular inclinations when stressed, and our stage of life.

When we are functioning in a state of anxiety-driven fusion, we may do any of the following things:

- we either distance ourselves from others, or seek them out and clutch them close to us;

- we either hold to our ideas, opinions, and positions rigidly, or appear to have none in a wishy-washy way;
- we tend to keep our real selves hidden, mostly out of mistrust of others and fear of disapproval;
- we avoid feedback or encouragement from others, or we deeply crave affirmation and support; or
- we insist on how different we are, or we resist any indication of differences.

The better differentiated we are, the more comfortable we are with either intense closeness or great distance from others without desperately craving or working to achieve either one.

What I mean by "closeness" is when two people in a family, a marriage, or a friendship can speak to each other in an open way. The degree of openness usually determines the level of closeness. This means that if we are close, I can say to you about any topic what I think, what I feel, what I want to do, or what I have done, and I do not get overly anxious about how you might react to me or judge me or tell me how I should be different. It also means that I can listen to you as you tell me these things about you and not react to you with evaluative comments and tell you how you should be different, or more like me.

For me, that is openness and closeness in a relationship. This allows for differences but also demonstrates a connection with one another. In addition, I can be emotionally comfortable enough when you are distant from me and do not want to, or cannot relate openly with me the way I would like. This would be like Elinor Dashwood in *Sense and Sensibility*, who had to endure Edward Ferrars's reserve and distance from her, and his lack of openness with her when earlier, he was closer and more open.

Sometimes **Austen's heroes have to endure being at great distances, emotionally and physically, from those they love**. The extreme example, of course, is Anne Elliot in *Persuasion* who endures nine years of separation from the man she loves with almost no hope that they will ever be together. When he reappears in her life, he maintains significant emotional distance and coolness. She manages to be comfortable with this and not pursue him.

The Comfort Zone

People will vary in how much closeness and distance they want in any particular relationship, at any particular time. Within a couple, a difference in how they prefer to act when one or both are anxious can itself become a problem. For example, when he is anxious, he tends to pull away; he goes silent and turns inward. She, on the other hand, when anxious moves toward him and wants to touch and talk. She wants reassurance.

Here is a diagram to show the close–distant comfort zones continuum from the point of view of the man's comfort level in this example. We could do a similar one for the woman. The comfort zone is where he can relate easily and be open. The "too close" or "too far" zones are when he can become anxious about the closeness or the distance with regard to some topic.

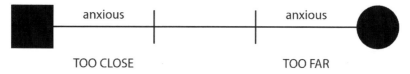

COMFORT ZONE

anxious | anxious

TOO CLOSE   TOO FAR

As we grow up in our families, we develop our comfort zones around closeness and distance. As totally dependent young infants, we desire only closeness and attention from our parents. In fact, as infants we believe our parents exist to serve our needs and should be there when we want them. Growing up is more or less about losing that belief. As we grow, we start experimenting with our individuality and getting some distance from them; we crawl and then walk to some other part of the room—with the parents still in the room. The distance causes some anxiety in our infant selves, which we are willing to endure for the pure joy of being "out there," on our own. Then we go back to them, in effect to touch the safe home base, and maybe get a hug or a caress, and then we are ready to go explore around the room again on our own.

This is all an exercise in learning whether we can cope with being out there on our own and still be safe. Initially, we don't want to get too far away. If the parents leave the room, we get a little more anxious and uneasy and can feel some sense of abandonment until they come back. If they don't come soon enough, we may start crying as a way to get them back. Eventually, we feel comfortable with that greater distance.

My mother told me that I only had one tantrum as a child, perhaps around the age of four. She was in a market shopping for food, when like all kids everywhere, I spotted something I wanted. She said no, so exercising my independence, I proceeded to throw a tantrum, lying down on the floor, kicking, and yelling—wanting my own way. Unembarrassed, Mom just walked away into another aisle of the grocery store. My safe home base was gone. She was not responding to my demands; there were just strangers around looking down at me. I shut down the tantrum and went looking for her, and I never did it again. **The fear of abandonment overcame my urge to demand that she do what I wanted.**

That same feeling can happen to us as adults. In our fusion, as I got older, if I ever got to the point of conflict with Mom, I could see her begin to go rigid and distant, and I shut up about what I wanted. No more tantrums. That is how we managed not to have a single verbal fight while I was growing up. Good or bad, that is how it worked. She was my only parent, and I did not want to lose her.

Therefore, I did not learn how to do conflict well in close relationships until I got married. When conflict developed between Lois and me early in the marriage, I would go silent and withdraw, as I did with Mom. I was pulling back into my personal comfort zone, and that was too far for Lois. She expected that we would talk or even argue about the issue at hand. It took me a long time to become comfortable with that, but it did happen. Eventually, I began to feel safer doing it. Arguing with her did not mean I was going to lose her.

We bring our closeness and distance patterns with us from our family of origin into whatever

new relationships we begin. I thought I was doing the right thing in refusing to talk about the differences, but Lois thought I was being unloving in doing so. To me, it seemed like the correct way to manage differences: it kept us calmer—I thought—and reduced the amount of upset—I thought. Actually, it was just a way to keep myself calmer and less anxious. In good relationships, the coming together and moving apart, just like dancing, happens easily and comfortably—both partners can tolerate both directions.

Pursuing and Distancing

A marriage may start with the two people seeming to have about the same level of comfort around closeness and distance, but often, fairly quickly in the relationship, one person will start being in charge of the closeness and the other being in charge of the distance. It will appear that one wants more closeness and the other more distance, and the roles of emotional pursuer and emotional distancer result. **When one distances, the other will pursue**, and the more distancing occurs, the more pursuit there is.

This is a common phenomenon. In a letter to her sister Cassandra, Austen tells about being at a ball where, "Mrs. B. thought herself obliged to leave [her group] to run around the room after her drunken husband. His avoidance, and her pursuit, with the probable intoxication of them both, was an amusing scene."

In this diagram, B is the emotional pursuer and A is the distancer. Then, at some point (see the next diagram), B gives up pursuing and starts to distance from A, feeling frustrated and unhappy. **If B distances enough, A begins to get anxious about B's distance.** Fearing abandonment, A starts moving toward B, wanting to make things better (the next diagram). Then when B responds to this, thinking maybe A has changed, B starts moving back toward him, at which point A starts distancing again (the next diagram). Again, the emotional pursuer feels confused or upset and maybe hurt— "same old story," she thinks.

**Then she distances in disappointment
and hurt, and he fears losing her**

anxious — fears abandonment

**She is encouraged by his move and
starts to move back toward him**

fears abandonment

**Hopeful again, she responds and pursues,
and he again retreats**

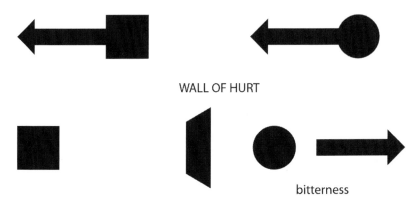

WALL OF HURT

bitterness

After this happens so many times, the pursuer retreats behind her wall of hurt and feels bitter and hopeless. The wall becomes permanent when a huge number of hurts and disappointments have occurred over the years. If they stay together, they can be stuck in this pattern into old age. If they go for counseling, they have a chance of changing it.

Pursuers think distancers have a problem with intimacy. Distancers think pursuers are too dependent. The issue, however, is fusion, having to agree and be the same in order to get along. When we get anxious, the patterns intensify in more extreme ways. The point of each one's behavior is that they are each attempting to reduce the intensity of their anxiety.

For example, the pursuer will be saying, "Talk to me more. Tell me what you are feeling." And the distancer, will be saying, in words or actions like walking out of the room or picking up the newspaper, "Leave me alone."

Each plays their part and they keep a balance that they are both most comfortable with.

If you don't believe this, here is an experiment you can try. If one of you changes his or her role and starts doing the opposite of what you normally do, a change will occur in the other. As the usual distancer in my relationship with Lois, when I learned about this pattern, I started being the pursuer, wanting to talk with her all of the time about everything, asking her, "What are you feeling now? What are you thinking? Where did you go? Who did you talk with? What are you going to do now? What was that experience like for you? Tell me all about it. I want to know everything going on with you." And of course, "Do you love me?" She quickly became the distancer, saying, "What's gotten into you? I don't want to talk right now. Leave me alone. Of course I love you. Shut up." We were keeping the same balance, just with the opposite roles. **So distancing and pursuing are not so much about personalities as about functional roles in relationships.**

It is hard for pursuers to become distancers in this exercise. I tell them they have not distanced enough if the former distancer has not started to pursue. If the other person really wants the relationship, they will start to pursue at some point. Remember, pursuers: distancers can always outdistance a pursuer. The distancer always wins, and most pursuers eventually learn this.

Good friends of ours had this pattern, with her as the pursuer and him as the distancer. She loved her husband, but she was never able to get the closeness she thought she wanted with him. Then he developed brain cancer and died. After a few years, she was ready to start dating again. She intentionally looked for a man who was comfortable with feelings and who was willing to talk with her about them. She found a nice man who liked to talk and was comfortable talking about his feelings. Not long into the marriage, she started to become the distancer. She found herself saying to him all of the things that her former husband had said to her. Then she got it: she did not need as much "closeness" as she had once thought. She told me that she could see the irony.

When these patterns become most problematic is when anxiety comes in: when there is some sense of threat around too much distance or too much closeness. When we are anxious about the closeness, **then we can feel swallowed up in the other, engulfed in them**, and losing self in them. If we thought while talking with the other person that it was just a general discussion of thoughts and feelings, telling each other about self, and not having to agree or debate the topic, or be the same as them, then we would be able to talk more openly. It is the anxiety about losing self in the fusion that inspires us to distance. This is a threat to our individuality. We all can feel this at certain points in a relationship.

If there is too much distance, we can feel abandoned. We think the other person's silence means they are not interested in us any more, or do not want us around. We think that maybe they want to leave us and be with someone else. This might even be the case, but when we pursue them constantly for reassurance, it usually does not work. We need to look at whether we are, in essence, asking them to give up who they are and be more like us. We all want to know we can be a self with the other. That always has a better chance of working.

One extreme version of distancing is the relationship nomad who can start relationships, but can never stay in ongoing relationships. The nomad shows a lot of impulsiveness around relationships. The nomad will lose interest and suddenly disappear. As a young man, I started in this direction, dating several girls and then dropping them. Marriage scared me partly because, growing up with just my mom, I never got to see how a married couple functions together. The relationship nomad will find "good" reasons to get out of each relationship and move on every time there is some disagreement or criticism.

You may never have thought of this before, but **criticism is one way we try to keep others close.** It is a form of pursuit. Of course, it usually backfires. In giving criticism, we want the other to be more the way we want them to be, to bring them closer to what we want in the sameness. This is the togetherness force at work. But the individuality of the other person feels rebuffed or put down, and distances as a result.

Jane Austen's Pursuers and Distancers

There are many examples of pursuers and distancers in Austen's novels. In *Pride and Prejudice*, Mr. Collins is the pursuer and Elizabeth Bennet is the distancer; conversely, Charlotte Lucas literally pursues Mr. Collins. Eventually Mr. Darcy pursues Elizabeth, and at first, she distances. Caroline Bingley shamelessly pursues Darcy, and he coolly distances. In *Sense and Sensibility*, Mr.

Willoughby is first the pursuer and then the distancer with Marianne Dashwood pursuing him. In *Mansfield Park*, Henry Crawford pursues Fanny Price, and she distances.

There are many, many more examples. Almost every page in Austen involves someone moving closer and someone else moving away. Anxiety, of some degree and type, is what usually inspires the movement.

Questions to Ponder

1. What have you learned about your own patterns of closeness and distance?

2. Are you typically more of a pursuer of others or a distancer from others? Can you remember times when you have done the opposite? Do you understand what your pattern is about for you? Is anxiety or a sense of threat involved?

3. Can you identify times with your partner or a good friend when things begin to feel either too close or too distant between you? How do you handle these times?

4. Do you ever feel so hurt that you put up a wall and refuse to connect with another person? Do you do this out of self-protection or out of punishment of the other? How well does that work to help you feel better?

7

Reacting to Our Differences

The main problem is not differences in points of view; it is the emotional reaction to the differences.

Michael Nichols

In chapter 17 of *Sense and Sensibility*, Elinor and Marianne Dashwood are discussing their difference in how they handle differences with others. Marianne thinks, mistakenly, that Elinor believes one should conform to or be guided by "the opinion of other people." This is partly because Elinor does not take every opportunity to point out how she differs from others. Marianne, on nearly every occasion, whatever the circumstances, whoever it is, says what she thinks, regardless of the impact on others. She reacts to others and actively differs with them whenever she feels the need.

"But I thought it was right, Elinor," said Marianne, "to be guided wholly by the opinion of other people. I thought our judgments were given us merely to be subservient to those of neighbours. This has always been your doctrine, I am sure."

"No, Marianne, never. My doctrine has never aimed at the subjection of the understanding. All I have ever attempted to influence has been the behaviour. You must not confound my meaning. I am guilty, I confess, of having often wished you to treat our acquaintance in general with greater attention; but when have I advised you to adopt their sentiments or to conform to their judgment in serious matters?"

"You have not been able, then, to bring your sister over to your plan of general civility," said Edward to Elinor, "Do you gain no ground?"

"Quite the contrary," replied Elinor, looking expressively at Marianne.

Marianne's is an intolerant individuality, and the ironic thing is that she wants others to agree with her. Hers is a pseudo-individuality; she is actually operating out of the fused togetherness force. What has her so deeply in love with Willoughby is that they appear to be exactly the same on every issue. She does not perceive that, chameleon-like, Willoughby is shaping himself to be what she wants for the sake of seduction.

It is normal in all relationships to have differences with others. This is primarily because of the force for individuality. We are all different. It is inevitable that we begin to think for ourselves, to have our own feelings, beliefs, and opinions. In relationships, the differences often become the focus of our difficulties. Under the influence of fusion and the togetherness force, one of us starts pushing the other to stop being different, to agree, and to do what we want. Then the other reacts to this push. Then push leads to shove. Elinor is gentle in her pushing Marianne, and Marianne has little to react to. If Elinor did push hard, however, there could be big fights between the sisters. Then their fights could overflow into the larger systems of family and friends. This kind of reactivity can run through a whole system. Bowen said, **"Emotional reactiveness in a family, or other group that lives or works together, goes from one family member to another in a chain reaction pattern."**

When we are less anxious, and the level of fusion is low, we can be together with others without needing them to be like us or do what we want. However, when the level of anxiety goes up, we tend to want others to be the way we want them to be (in thinking, or feelings, or actions), or conversely, we may be willing to give up self and to submit ourselves to them and their wishes. The better differentiated we are, the better we can deal with these processes and not be done in by them emotionally. The more we feel emotionally infringed upon by the other reveals our level of fusion with the other. Reactivity reveals our fusion with the other.

If the people involved are relatively mature, and less fused, then the differences are not a threat (that is, not a cause for anxiety), and there is no problem. They are just different, and they can figure out how to live with the differences in a civil way. This can involve any issue or any personal preference. For most couples, some differences are no big deal: you say "tomayto" and I say "tomahto." Their individuality is okay.

Maybe we see our partner, or our child, or a friend doing something that we think is wrong. With some level of anxiety in us, we criticize them, or plead, cajole, seduce, or manipulate them to conform to our wishes. And you don't often hear people respond to a criticism by saying, "Well, that is an interesting idea you have about how I should be. I can appreciate that you think it will bring us closer together if I become more how you want me to be. Let's talk about that." Instead, **we begin a reactive dance of universal patterned ways to deal with the emotional pressures for conformity** in the conflict.

Common Relationship Patterns of Reactivity

Dr. Bowen described the basic patterns of reactivity that he observed repeatedly in relationships. Austen also shows them to us in her books. Here are the common, universal patterns for dealing with the push for sameness, or responding to criticism, which is a disguised push for sameness.

Emotional Distancing

Emotional distancing is an integral component of each of the other forms of reactivity listed below. When distancing, we are being less open or revealing of ourselves. We distance when we think that the relationship cannot tolerate openness and we wish to keep things calm, or to keep ourselves calm. For example, many families have a rule against talking about religion or politics. They maintain emotional distance on these topics.

Bowen said distancing is "the most universal mechanism" for dealing with anxiety. It is present in all relationships to some degree. We are rarely entirely open with the other with what we think. As Austen said in *Emma*, "Seldom, very seldom, does complete truth belong to any human disclosure; seldom can it happen that something is not a little disguised or a little mistaken."

We all know how to distance. We started doing it as little kids. At some point, we all stopped telling our parents everything we thought, felt, or had done because they criticized or punished us for it. We all have a certain amount of conflict avoidance in us whether it is out of politeness, fear of fighting, or as in what Elinor Dashwood says to her sister in the passage above, "civility." Open conflict is uncomfortable for many of us, so we may just ignore the issue, smile and say nothing, or move on to something else: the ways we do this avoiding are unending.

For example, children who have grown up and left home may only infrequently contact their parents or respond to their overtures. They distance emotionally as well as physically. They are done with parents who evaluate them and tell them who they ought to be, or how to act in life. The parents often deal with this distancing with more criticism to inspire guilt, which only inspires the adult child to distance even more. And when we feel guilty, we usually distance.

We can distance from another person physically by walking out of the room or out of the house or by becoming engaged in a hobby or activity. We can distance emotionally while in the same room by picking up the paper or a book, turning on the TV, or even while apparently engaged in a conversation with the other, by just not saying what we really think. **We may do this so habitually that we have no idea how even to know what we think, let alone how to say it.** We are just disengaged. We go along to get along, but it isn't really getting along.

Sometimes we distance out of hurt. We think that to engage the other and discuss our differences would hurt even more. When Marianne Dashwood discovered Willoughby's faithlessness, she drew away from others, including her own family, wanting to be alone. She did not want to talk about the hurt. In effect, however, she ended up nurturing the hurt, which made it worse for her. She was so withdrawn that she got sick and nearly died.

In a close relationship, instead of talking about our differences, we may avoid them by gossiping or talking about other people, the children, the pet, politics, or whatever. Talking about others is a good way to distance from the one we are with. This way we can look engaged and even appear to be close to the other (when we agree about the gossip), while avoiding talking openly about self, self's experience in life, thinking, or our experience with the other.

Plenty can be going on inside us that we do not talk about. One friend had his wife leave him after five years of marriage. She just moved out, taking their two kids, and disappeared with no warning. She left behind a written list on the dining table of all of her grievances and complaints about him. She had never raised them with him in a serious way while she was with him. She saw him as the problem, and she was getting away from him as a solution to the problem.

This is what we are usually doing when we distance. I know that my friend could be somewhat pushy, opinionated, and demanding in a relationship. Clearly, his wife did not know how to engage or fight with him over her issues. She distanced into silence and resentment, and finally, she left him. He was dumbfounded and felt powerless.

This is an example of the way many people spend a lot of time internally thinking about the relationship, usually with a great deal of resentment or perhaps fear, but they may never verbalize their concerns. Early on in *Mansfield Park*, Fanny Price distances out of anxiety and fear. She does not want to fight with anyone, and she doesn't dare say what she really thinks for fear of rejection. However, as the story develops, Fanny slowly learns to speak up for herself and do less emotional distancing.

Open Conflict

There are two types of open conflict. In the first type, couples openly fight about their differences, whatever they are. With some couples who do this, it seems as if any topic will lead to a fight. Many of these couples are hard to be around because they seem to fight all of the time. Their friends and often their kids wonder why they stay together. These people are George and Martha of *Who's Afraid of Virginia Woolf?* or Richard Burton and Elizabeth Taylor as they were reputed to be—which made their fights in the film version of the play so believable.

They each demand that the other agree with them and insist that the other is wrong or at fault. **There is a great deal of criticism by each of them about the other one**. Neither can listen well to the other, nor concede that the other has any valid points. They will not look for the part in the other's position that they can agree with. They can't find common ground or find a way to compromise.

At the marital level, these couples are exactly like the polarized parties in our politics. They can do a great deal of blaming the other for the things that go wrong. They say, "It's all your fault! Don't blame me. You are the one who is screwing things up and who has to change." The other partner says the same thing and gives evidence for why he or she is right. They can become very bitter and are capable of hurting each other significantly with words and sometimes physically. As Austen says in *Pride and Prejudice*, "Angry people are not always wise."

The second type of open conflict is adolescent rebellion (which sometimes appears in an adult rebel who acts like an adolescent). The adolescent rebel refuses to do what the authority wants done—whatever that is. Lydia Bennet in *Pride and Prejudice* is somewhat like this, and this behavior pattern contributes to her impulsive running away with Wickham. **The rebel is trying to show they are their own person by refusing to go along with what the other wants.** They say, "You can't tell me what to do! I am grown up and can do what I want."

In fact, the authority still controls them. They are just doing the opposite of what the authority wants; the authority is still in charge. They usually find someone to play along and be the authority so they can rebel. Because they are not thinking that well for themselves, they often make poor decisions and get themselves in trouble, finding, as a result, more authorities who will challenge them.

Open conflict is still about emotional distancing, even though those involved are heatedly engaging one another. In conflict, we focus on criticizing the other, not on being open about self. To be open about self will feel too vulnerable, so we attack what we think is the vulnerability of the other, and the other does the same to us. And on it goes with cycles of defense and attack.

Compliance

One form of emotional distancing and refusal to deal with differences or conflict is compliance, or apparent compliance. Frank Churchill in *Emma* does this with his parents by not telling them about his secret engagement to Jane Fairfax. He wants to maintain the appearance of compliance with what they want. This secret keeps Jane in a kind of emotional limbo, since she cannot let others know about the engagement and has to act like there is no one in her life. Clearly, she becomes depressed around this loss of self.

Employees may comply with their bosses, and often this is a wise strategy. However, in *Pride and Prejudice*, we see the price of compliance. The Reverend Mr. Collins conforms to the wishes of Lady Catherine, who is his benefactor in providing him with a parish stipend. He toadies to her, adopting her values, beliefs, and opinions like a puppet. He keeps any potential anxiety at bay by doing this, but if he really stood up for the beliefs of his church, he could not possibly think the same way she does. He just sets those beliefs aside to stay in her good graces.

In some marriages, one partner may normally be the dominant decision-maker, and the other partner appears to adapt or comply and go along. But the compliant partner may find ways to subvert the other's decisions through apparent ignorance, stupidity, or uncertainty, or by being forgetful or clumsy, or by having some disability. **The joke about how to have a happy marriage is that you just keep saying, "Yes, dear."**

These couples never openly fight or recognize their differences. The compliant partner can pretend that there are no differences and that the two are the same. Or the compliant partner can take the passive-aggressive strategy of always saying, "Yes, dear," but then never doing what is agreed to or doing it so poorly that it has to be done again.

The "peace at any price" relationship does not attempt to deal with important differences and conflict. However, avoiding conflict does not really reduce the intensity of fusion in the relationship. It just means the conflict is not so openly displayed. Doing a lot of conflict avoidance will lead to the "walking on eggshells" experience in a relationship.

The continually compliant person often ends up being depressed, or they may get physically sick and for some reason be unable to function in their role as partner. There are several forms of depression, but the type I dealt with most often in my practice was this conflict-avoidant person. With these depressed people, eventually I would ask them, "To whom do you give up self?" The depression usually lifted when the person stopped giving up self to that other person, like a married partner. However, then marital conflict would break out, when the compliant person began to claim his or her own self in the relationship.

Under-Functioning and Over-Functioning Reciprocity

Under-functioning and over-functioning reciprocity is a common variation of compliance that shows up as a pattern of behavior in the two partners together. Some compliant people (the under-functioners in this pattern) emotionally drop out of the marriage. They may find some activity or hobby outside the home that they pursue with energy and gusto, but back at home they become a no-self and display none of that energy. Or they may under-function everywhere and take little responsibility for self anywhere.

Over-functioners have lots of energy to do things for others, even when they are not asked

to do so. They see what they think is a problem, and they set out to fix it, unaware that they might be stepping on someone's toes in the process. How could anyone possibly want to decline their help? They are good at finding under-functioners and trying to help them do better in life. They do not realize that by doing so they are encouraging more under-functioning. As Austen said in *Emma*, "There are people, who the more you do for them, the less they will do for themselves." Mrs. Grant in *Mansfield Park* over-functions in the family as a whole, but especially for the two young daughters. They grow up with a highly privileged and irresponsible attitude because they are used to her doing everything for them.

Physical, Emotional, or Social Dysfunction in One Family Member

When the over- and under-functioning pattern is very strong, a family member may show physical, emotional, or social dysfunction. Under-functioners give up self, and over-functioners gains self. As self decreases in the adaptive person, they become more vulnerable to stress, their level of anxiety increases, and eventually some symptoms may emerge. These symptoms can be a physical illness, an emotional illness such as depression, or some kind of social acting out such as drinking to excess or getting in trouble with the law. When this happens, the adaptive "sick" family member may be sent to some practitioner who is supposed to help such people. They may be sent to a medical doctor or a therapist, or they might become involved with the police and the courts. My uncle Wallace was a heavy drinker. He had trouble functioning adequately. His father, my grandfather, as the over-functioner, always bailed him out of difficulties and tried to control his drinking, but with little success. As the above quote from Austen describes, the more my grandfather did for Wallace, the less Wallace did for himself.

The over-functioning partner will be more knowledgeable, able to get things done, be successful in most endeavors undertaken, and be the apparently most competent and responsible member. The adaptive "sick" one will have less ability to think and act for self in a responsible way. Mary Musgrove in *Persuasion* is a good example of an under-functioning family member: she is a wife and mother who often feels ill or is unable to cope, so that others step in and take on her responsibilities.

The adaptive under-functioners may look like they are the "problem" in the relationship. The couple will look significantly mismatched in that one is so competent and the other so incompetent. Looking at these couples, one often wonders what drew them together. Wherever there is an under-functioner, you will usually find one or more over-functioners. In my practice, families or couples would try to present the under-functioning person for therapy, to get me to "fix" them because they couldn't. Instead, I always chose to work with the over-functioners. They are the ones who have the most ability and motivation to change. The under-functioner will not change if the over-functioner will not change. Period.

It is often said that we have to delegate responsibility to others, but when we try to delegate to under-functioners, it often fails. The act of delegation itself is a way of over-functioning. In these cases, **we have to delegate anxiety**. Over-functioners are the ones who carry the anxiety in the relationship. If they can let go of that anxiety, eventually the under-functioner will get it. In *Emma*, Mr. Knightley has a strong tendency to over-function with Emma. He has been doing it for a long time, since she was a young girl. He has to learn to step back and let her experience the consequences of her foolishness.

When the anxiety shifts to the under-functioner, it can be a motivator. When someone becomes anxious for their own life and well-being, then they will be motivated to do something about it. But not until then. **This is the positive function of anxiety: it gets us moving.**

My mother just never got anxious or took responsibility for how I should run my life. There were certainly times when she could have, but she was never on my case. I got the message loud and clear that if I was going to go anywhere in life, it was up to me. I always got my own jobs. She never once prodded or pushed me toward anything. I was not a serious student in high school, but then in my junior year of college, I realized I had to be a better student to get where I wanted to go. I decided I had to work at my studies and stop just having fun. I felt the anxiety about my future and took responsibility for it.

I did not stop under-functioning entirely. Here is one example of my under-functioning as a married man. **What is the one wedding gift that husbands most often give to their brides? It is their mother.** I have mentioned that I had distanced from my mother, and when Lois and I married, I maintained that distance.

I expected, without actually saying so, that Lois would look after the relationship with her. For the first two years of marriage, Lois bought the birthday cards and the Christmas gifts and made the phone calls. I did nothing—with my own mother!

Then one day, in a self-differentiating move, Lois said to me, "You know, I have my own mother that I do these things for, and I don't need to do them for you. From now on, I will initiate nothing with regard to your mother, and I am not going to bug you about it. If something happens, it will be up to you. If nothing happens, that will be your choice as well." She stopped over-functioning for me. There was no anger in her saying this. There was no rebellion, or blaming, or evaluating me as a lousy son or anything like that. She just defined her self to me and stated the fact of what she would and mostly would not do.

I didn't say anything, but there was a hollow feeling in my stomach because I knew she was serious. I tested her anyway, not intentionally so much as by inaction and uncertainty about how to proceed. For over two years, I continued to initiate nothing with my mother. Practically no phone calls, letters, cards, or gifts. Lois never said anything to me about my inaction. Saying something would be over-functioning. She did not try to cajole me into doing something. She just dropped it and never mentioned my inaction.

This was the best thing she could do. Gradually, I decided I had to do something, although this took over two years. Slowly, I started moving toward my mother, and that turned out to be a wonderful thing. So much good came from that. I began a long, rewarding process of connecting with her. I finally began feeling and acting like a loving and caring son who did appreciate his mother. We became more emotionally open and involved with one another. When my mother died, I felt that I had done my best with her and had let her know through my words and actions that I loved her, which I did. It happened only because Lois stopped taking responsibility for my relationship with her.

Telling people what they should do, repeatedly, is taking responsibility for them. You can say it once, maybe twice, but then leave it to them. Think how hard it had to be for Lois in a context where the cultural norm is for the wife to take responsibility for the connection with her husband's mother. The loss of contact and initiative looked like her fault; as if she was an uncaring wife and daughter-in-law. She differentiated herself from me, but at some cost to her image with my mother although, as usual, Mom never said anything.

Projection to a Child

Often couples will avoid their own conflicts by focusing on a child who seems to be having problems. **They make a cause out of their child rather than out of their marriage, or their own life.** Whenever parents presented their child as the problem in therapy, I would soon have the parents in and get them to address the issues between them.

Questions to Ponder

1. What were your standard patterns of reactivity while growing up in your family of origin?
2. What are your patterns in your relationships today?
3. Would you like to change any of your patterns of reactivity?
4. When others are reactive to you, how do you understand that, and what do you think is your part in that process?

8

The Sibling Relationship and Good Relationships

Never praise a sister to a sister, in the hope of your compliments reaching the proper ears.
Rudyard Kipling

tenants of life's middle state,
Securely placed between the small and great
William Cowper

Being an only child is a disease in itself.
Stanley Hall

What is the longest relationship you will have in your life? It is with your siblings. Depending on your sibling position, they will know you in your earliest days and may be there when you grow old. Your sibling posi-

127

tion is about whether you come first, middle, or last in the order of your birth and whether you are male or female. No one else in your life will have known you for as long and have as good an understanding of what your early, formative years were like. After your parents, your relationship with your siblings, whether it is good or bad, will have one of the greatest impacts on your life. For many people, having their siblings around in old age is a real joy.

In *Mansfield Park* (chapter 24), Austen puts "fraternal ties" above "conjugal" ties. "Children of the same family, the same blood, with the same first associations and habits, have some means of enjoyment in their power, which no subsequent connections can supply." She says that we never outlive these attachments even if the relationship in later life is not a happy one.

The growing-up relationship with our brothers and sisters is where we first begin to learn about love (and hate), and other issues like cooperation, tolerance, and developing the skills of leadership, assertiveness, and negotiation.

Your own sex and your ordinal position in the family has a lot to say about how your own personality develops. It affects your marriage, your parenting style, your general functioning in your adult relationships, and how your life course develops. This may sound like too strong a statement but there is a good bit of science to back it up.

Several studies have shown that having siblings that we maintain contact with as we age is good for our health. One study says it adds about seven and a half years to our lives, about the same as being a non-smoker. A Swedish study found that contact with one's siblings in one's eighties correlated with a positive mood and general satisfaction with life. Another study, done by Harvard's Dr. George Vaillant, followed a group of men from their college days onward, beginning in the 1940s. The **men who were physically and mentally the healthiest in their old age were those who had good relationships with their siblings in their early twenties**.

Dr. Walter Toman, an Austrian psychologist, realized that traditional psychological theory said a lot about the impact of parents on children, but practically nothing about how siblings affected a child's development and personality. Freud did note that "a child's position in the sequence of brothers and sisters is of very great significance for the course of his later life," but he did nothing further with this observation.

Toman studied two large samples of couples (2,300 couples each in Austria and in Massachusetts) to arrive at his data. The couples were non-clinical, that is, they were not in treatment for marital or child therapy. As a result of his study, he was able to make some significant generalizations about the personalities of people in the different sibling positions. Since his work, others, like Dr. Alfred Adler, have made similar observations about sibling characteristics.

Not all of us fit our birth order profile as described in this literature. Bowen adopted Toman's work and clarified the reasons why some of us do not fit the usual description. These reasons have to do primarily with family emotional processes that Bowen considered but that Toman did not take into account. These two men became friends in later life, and Toman adopted Bowen's views on emotional process. Toman's work is the only concept Bowen took into his theory from outside his own observational work. Bowen said that **"No single piece of data is more important than knowing the sibling position of people."**

There is not enough room here to describe all of the sibling positions and how birth order affects personality. Lois and I describe the theory and the various birth order profiles in depth in our book called *Birth Order and You: How Your Sex and Position in the Family Affects Your Personality, Career, Relationships, and Parenting*. We include comments on the traits of many famous contemporary personalities and how their sibling position affected them and their careers as adults.

It has been known through the centuries in popular culture that oldest children and youngest children each had some characteristics in common. Toman's work refined and formalized these popular notions with hard data. In my therapy practice, I would often explain to couples and families some of the sibling position characteristics. It would be illuminating for them to hear: "This is just the way an oldest brother tends to behave. It is not about you. He is not this way because of his feelings, or lack thereof, for you." After reading our book on birth order profiles, clients said to me "How did you know me so well?—the description fits me to a T." Or their partner would say it.

When Lois and I first read the descriptions for our positions as an only female and an only male child, it clarified many of the fights we had. **It was as if the words in some of our disagreements were scripted long ago in our sibling position.** Once we understood that some behavior patterns were characteristic of our birth position, we could stop personalizing that behavior as being caused by the other's feelings for us.

Here is an example of the power of birth position. Lois and I decided not to have children. We finalized this decision only after extensive discussions over a ten-year period. Twice, we even drew up very rational lists of the pros and cons for us having children. This was not about attitudes toward other people having children, just us. Later on, we read Toman. He said, "When two only children marry each other they often decide not to have children." We were amazed. So much for our rationality. It was in our sibling positions.

Austen herself knew the importance of siblings. All of her heroes have them, and they rely on them to varying degrees; most often in her books, sisters are best friends with each other. The way she describes the siblings' behavior fits quite well with birth order theory. As an oldest brother, Darcy is not used to being teased, or laughed at. His younger sister Georgiana was surprised that Elizabeth could do this and get away with it.

Even Austen, in her relationship with her older sister Cassandra, appears to fit the descriptions quite well. She was a younger sister of a sister and of brothers. She also has some qualities of an older sister of a brother. Her relationships with her brothers clearly informed much of her writing about men and the relationships between men and women. These brothers were also her entrée into the larger culture. Through them, she learned more about the world beyond than what most women were allowed to experience in their own right.

Birth order theory does not say what anyone should be like. It is descriptive, not prescriptive. **No position is better than another. All positions have strengths and weaknesses attached to them.** Whether a person shows the more positive or negative characteristics typical of their birth order position depends in part on their level of emotional maturity or differentiation. More emotionally mature people demonstrate the more positive aspects of their position, while more immature people demonstrate the more the negative aspects. For example, oldests can be either more sensitive or caring toward their younger siblings, or they can be more dictatorial and demanding of them.

I had one seventy-year-old volunteer in my office doing typing. She was a young-in-spirit seventy: always the life of the party, always joking and fun. She was the youngest of five girls, and when she read the description for her birth position, she said, "Yep, that's me." In her social life and work relationships—even though she always worked with people much younger than her—she said, "I am always the youngest, whoever I am with." She saw some negatives in that as well as the positives.

The Ten Basic Sibling Positions

Here are the ten basic sibling positions. Each one has a corresponding personality description.

1. Oldest brother of brothers
2. Oldest brother of sisters
3. Youngest brother of brothers
4. Youngest brother of sisters
5. Oldest sister of sisters
6. Oldest sister of brothers
7. Youngest sister of sisters
8. Youngest sister of brothers
9. Only male and only female children
10. Twins

The Middle Child

You will note that I have left middle children out of this list. Since going unnoticed is their experience of life in general, they often take umbrage with this approach, but the reason there is no specific description of the middle child position is that there are so many variations.

The characteristics of a middle child will depend mostly on which sibling they were the closest to growing up. When there are more than two siblings in a family, they tend to break up into smaller groups, usually depending on the difference in their ages. If there is a gap of four or five years in age between an older sibling and the middle child that follows, then the middle child is usually closer to the siblings that are born afterward, giving them a role that is more like the oldest of the siblings below them. If that middle child is closer to the siblings who are older, then they are more like a younger sibling. It depends on which siblings they spent the most time with while growing up. Most often, the middle child can have a mix of positions, spending time with both older and younger siblings, and this gives them the extra advantage of being able to understand more points of view, especially if the other siblings are of different sexes. As adults, they often become negotiators or moderators between people with conflicting viewpoints.

Sometimes the middle child just gets lost. In *Pride and Prejudice*, Mary, the middle of five daughters in the Bennet family did not have a very close relationship with either the two older sisters or the two younger sisters. She developed a closer relationship with books, and this left her somewhat out of step socially. In the various family situations that occurred, she would offer some quote from her reading that was vaguely related to the situation but often inappropriate. The family did not take her seriously even though she was a serious young girl. At the end of the book, after all of her sisters were gone from home, Austen says Mary began to prosper somewhat "as she was no longer mortified" by comparisons with her sisters.

Other Factors in Understanding One's Position

This sibling position concept helps us to understand why it is that children born in the same family, who share 50 percent of their genes, can end up being so different from each other. In fact, they work hard to define themselves differently from their siblings. This is part of what sibling theory helps explain. The result of the force for individuality and the emotional process in families leads each child to want their own distinctive identity. In addition, they develop their own ways of relating to other family members around levels of closeness and openness or greater distance and lack of connection.

The differences also relate to the family circumstances at the time of birth. **Children are never, except in the case of twins, born into the same family.** The circumstances of the family when each child is born can differ quite a bit, in a huge variety of ways. Families change through time, from year to year. If you have siblings, just think about what was different in the life of the family when you were born and they were born. One major difference, of course, is the presence or not of other siblings.

The loss of a parent through either death or divorce, and the subsequent remarriage and "blending" of families also creates a different family environment that later children are born into. The early death of a sibling and of other important family members can have major impact on sibling development. If there are adoptions, or if a sibling has a disability, that will have an impact that affects personality development for all involved. The level of anxiety in the family around each birth is a major factor, and this can vary over time.

For a variety of reasons, parents do often have favorite children, and they develop closer relationships with those children. Mrs. Bennet in *Pride and Prejudice* clearly feels closer to her two youngest daughters. Austen indicates that part of the reason for this is that she is trying to relive her own youth when she was an attractive young woman who enjoyed the attention of men. This was her position in her own family of origin, and it leads her to be a less responsible parent.

One of the major factors in personality development is whether the parents focus their anxiety on a particular child. Bowen theory calls this the family projection process. Often such a child will have a quite skewed version of their more typical sibling position. Even though he was an only child, this process was a major factor in my cousin Tom's life.

Sibling Position and Marriage

In marriage, **couples can be complementary or conflictual in terms of their sibling rank (oldest, middle, or youngest) and their sex (male or female)**. For example, an oldest brother of brothers married to an oldest sister of sisters will have both a rank and a sex conflict. As two oldests, being of the same rank, they are both used to being in charge and calling the shots, so they both may want to take charge and have different views of "what should be done" in any particular situation. That is a rank conflict. Having grown up only with siblings of the same sex, they will have less understanding of the opposite sex. That is a sex conflict. On the other hand, an oldest brother of sisters married to a younger sister of brothers will have no rank or sex conflict. They will tend to be complementary in both aspects of their relationship.

This single fact has an impact on divorce rates. **Sibling position can significantly affect the amount of conflict and the outcome of a marriage.** Toman, in his research, was able to verify this as he looked at the divorce rate of various couples. In his samples, the combination that had the highest rate of divorce (37 percent) was, as predicted, an oldest brother of brothers married to an oldest sister of sisters. In some cases, however, if they have the ability to deal maturely with each other, these couples can make tremendous marriages and raise extremely competent children.

The divorce rate for marriages between an oldest brother of sisters and a youngest sister of brothers was, as predicted, 0 percent. There were no divorces in either of his two samples, which added up to 4,600 couples. In this combination, each partner has a good understanding of the opposite sex, and each is more used to the arrangement of who is in charge in the relationship. This arrangement works well until, for example, the husband gets tired of having a more dependent wife, or the wife rebels against his authority and wants to be more her own person. I have had people in both of these situations as clients.

The second most problematic marriage combination in Toman's research was two onlies married to each other (such as Lois and me): their divorce rate was 21 percent. Again, the outcome depends on the couple's level of maturity. Only children share many of the characteristics of oldests and are used to running their lives in their own way. For example, it is more difficult for them to share, or to negotiate compromises. It is also more difficult for only children to adapt to the other's way of doing things. In addition, they grow up not knowing or understanding all that much about the opposite sex. Thus, they have both a rank and sex conflict.

Other Sibling Issues

Our birth order can also affect the way we parent. Oldest children and youngest children tend to become quite different kinds of parents. I mentioned earlier the difference in the parenting style of my mother's older sister with her only child (my cousin Tom) compared to my mother, the younger sister, with me. Their different styles of parenting had a significant impact on our life courses. Other important family emotional processes were involved, like the level of anxiety and emotional fusion, but the sibling position of each mother was a significant part of it.

Sibling position can strongly affect a person's work life. How they relate to their boss is one example. Lois and I both got along well with all of our bosses, and they liked us. As only children, we grew up living more in the world of adults. Our focus in life was on them, rather than on siblings, and we learned quickly how to negotiate our relationships with adults in authority. Oldest children, as adults, have a harder time taking orders or agreeing with the boss's plans or direction. I always wanted oldests as my office managers. They were very efficient and organized and got the job done. However, I had to be careful how I gave orders for doing the work, and I couldn't be too rigid about how they should do their job. One time, I forgot this and ended up in a big shouting match with my office manager.

One's position will also help determine who we will get along with the best and the worst as coworkers in the office setting. Just like in marriage, there are better and less good fits between people in the office. When some people have almost automatic reactions to coworkers that either draw them to each other or repel them from each other, often sibling position and the past experience with a sibling is the underlying issue. If the less mature, more negative characteristics are present in a person, then there can be definite conflicts between coworkers.

Questions to Ponder

At the end of our birth order book, we give many questions that siblings can use to interview each other about their experience in the family. These questions have proved useful to many people. The siblings learn more about each other, and they understand their own life in their family better. Here are just a few of these questions.

1. Which of your siblings were you closest to while growing up, and how do you think that affected your own development?
2. Which ones are you closest to now, and which ones are you more distant from? Would you like to change that at all?
3. What impact do you think you had on your own siblings? Have you talked with them about this?
4. Were you happy with your sibling position?
5. If you have a parent who had the same sibling position as you, have you ever talked about that and compared notes?

9

The Key to Making
Good Relationships

**A dead thing can go with the stream, but only a
living thing can go against it.**

G. K. Chesterton

The core issue in making good relationships is the Bowen
theory concept of differentiation of self. It is the key to
emotional maturity. Bowen said that differentiation of
self is the cornerstone of his theory, and while Austen
obviously never used the term "differentiation," her work
shows it as the most important characteristic of her heroes. Elizabeth Bennet is the best example, but each of
the other heroes also demonstrates this important quality
to some extent. In her dramatic encounter with Lady
Catherine de Bourgh in chapter 56 of *Pride and Preju-*

dice, Elizabeth's emotional maturity allows her to take the stand that she does.

In that scene, Lady Catherine makes a surprise visit to the Bennet household, driving up in her "chaise and four," which would be the equivalent today of arriving in a Rolls-Royce. She behaves abruptly and rudely, demanding to talk with Elizabeth. She has heard of a possible marriage between Darcy and Elizabeth. This is news to Elizabeth; Darcy has made no new proposal and, although his demeanor toward her has changed, she had no clue he might renew his wish to marry her. Elizabeth herself has indeed reconsidered him after visiting Darcy's country estate of Pemberley, accidently meeting him there, and getting an entirely different picture of him. Lady Catherine believes this rumor of a marriage must be "a scandalous falsehood" and has come to get Elizabeth's promise not to marry Darcy. She accuses Elizabeth of using her "arts and allurements" to draw him in and "make him forget what he owes to himself and all his family." She also falsely claims that he is engaged to her own daughter.

Under such an onslaught, Elizabeth manages to keep her cool and is able to question and reason with Lady Catherine on each point that she raises. Even though Lady Catherine continues to insult her and demands that Elizabeth promises not to marry Darcy, Elizabeth says, "I will make no promise of the kind." Lady Catherine pulls out all the stops. She refers to what she thinks is the bad reputation of Elizabeth's family, saying finally, "Are the shades of Pemberley to be thus polluted?" and calling Elizabeth an "unfeeling, selfish girl," she makes various more threats and storms back to her carriage.

Lady Catherine's focus is entirely on Elizabeth, and she tries to intimidate her into complying, as she does with everyone else in her life. Her focus is on what "you" should do and not do and on defining what a bad person "you" are. Elizabeth only defines herself to Lady Catherine, reasoning with her and questioning some of her assumptions, and saying what she herself will or will not do. She does not react in kind and call Lady Catherine names. She does not say, "You are a rude, terrible person. You have no right to barge into my house and make demands of me," or any other such comment that we might be tempted to make. Defining self is a key element in differentiation.

Differentiation of self is the only concept in Bowen theory that focuses on the individual, but we can only understand it fully within the context of the other concepts discussed in the previous chapters. It is about the essential strength it takes to build good relationships. One definition of differentiation is this one from Bowen: **"A differentiated self is one who can maintain emotional objectivity while in the midst of an emotional system in turmoil, yet at the same time actively relate to key people in the system."**

Mostly, Elizabeth keeps her objectivity and keeps relating to a very objectionable woman. She does not distance. Elizabeth maintains contact with her. Lady Catherine is the one who finally distances. The concept of differentiation is primarily about who we are and then secondly, about a way of being with others. Another leader in Bowen theory, Dan Papero, put it this way: "Differentiation is about how people differ from one another in terms of their sensitivity to one another and their varying abilities to preserve a degree of autonomy in the face of the pressure for togetherness." This encounter illustrates this perfectly.

The more sensitive we are to how others are, the more fused we are with them. Differentiation is about stepping out of the fusion with others and how they are and being more focused on being a self with them. Even if others are highly critical of us and push us to be the way they want, we can stay faithful to our goals for how we want to be with them, and in life generally, especially during times of upset and higher anxiety. **Differentiation is not about how we want others to be with us.**

Clearly, some of us are much better at being this way on a consistent basis than are others. Our level of fused sensitivity to the other can lead us to react to them rather than more autonomously defining our self to them. Even if just one person in an emotional system manages to achieve a moderately higher level of differentiation, or keep a connection with the system, people in the system as a whole will do better.

The Inner and the Outer

Differentiation has two aspects to it: an inner one and an outer one. Inner differentiation has to do with how well we separate thinking and feeling; outer differentiation has to do with how well we maintain an unreactive position with others. They are two sides of the same coin. In both aspects, a lack of differentiation implies fusion.

Inwardly, we all experience more or less fusion between our thinking and feelings. **The more fused we are with others, the more our thinking is run by our feelings.** This would be Marianne Dashwood in *Sense and Sensibility*. This is less true of her sister Elinor. This does not mean Elinor is without feelings. Her feelings are just as powerful as Marianne's, but she is better able to stay true to her goals for how she wants to be with others in spite of how she is feeling. As Austen describes Elinor, "She had an excellent heart; her disposition was affectionate and her feelings were strong; but she knew how to govern them. . . ." When feeling and thinking are more fused, we tend to make our subjective feelings into objective facts. Even though Willoughby had never proposed to her, Marianne *felt* engaged to him, and made her feelings into a fact. Marianne's feelings governed her.

Outwardly, better differentiation means there is less fusion with others, less reactivity to them, and therefore we are better able to relate to them, even when they are highly reactive to us. Marianne is highly fused with Willoughby. When she discovers his faithlessness, her reaction nearly destroys her. Her major loss of self in the fusion leads her into a deep depression and even a physical illness that brings her near death. Elinor also experiences loss, finding out that Edward is secretly engaged to Lucy Steele, but her greater differentiation of self allows her to stay on an even keel. Even though she is sad, this does not become depression. Her feelings do not run her life.

Bowen theory recognizes the wide variation across the spectrum of emotional maturity. People fall on a continuum from highly fused to well differentiated. We could imagine a line going from 0 percent differentiation, or totally fused, to 100 percent differentiated. The diagram below shows the inner and outer aspects of differentiation as well: the inner aspect is the fusion or differentiation between feeling and thinking in ourselves, and the outer aspect is the fusion or differentiation between self and other.

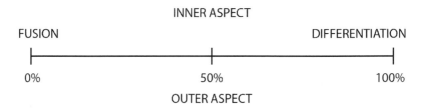

No one is totally fused or totally differentiated. Most of us are below 50 percent differentiated—50 percent would actually be very good. A person who was beyond 75 percent differentiated would be very unusual in human history to this point. I would put myself at around 38 percent on this scale. On occasion, I can function at a higher level, but when I get anxious my level of differentiation won't get much higher than this.

The encounter between Lady Catherine and Elizabeth Bennet represents the different ends of the continuum. Lady Catherine is highly fused with her family (outer aspect) and feels (inner aspect) tremendously responsible for her vision of the family's good name. She is doing what she thinks is necessary to uphold the family name, to protect her daughter's interests, and to keep the estate of Pemberley from being "polluted" by Darcy marrying someone more common like Elizabeth.

Her feelings run her thinking, showing her inner fusion. In her outer fusion, she thinks she can demand the behavior she wants from others and get their assent. She wants them to fit in with her beliefs about what is right, like Mr. Collins does. She reacts strongly when others do not go along with her wishes. Most often people in her circle have complied.

Elizabeth, while quite surprised by this assault from Lady Catherine, is able to hang on to her self, not be caught up in the fusion and reactivity for the most part, and to define herself to Lady Catherine. She refuses to promise to Lady Catherine that she will not marry Darcy. Neither she nor Lady Catherine knows that in doing this she is also sending a positive message to Darcy about her feelings for him. He, surreptitiously, has helped set up this scene by informing Lady Catherine of his intentions.

While the relationship with Lady Catherine does not look promising at the moment, Elizabeth is the one at the end of the book who persuades Darcy to reconnect with her and re-involve her in their family life. This is a further sign of her higher level of differentiation. She is not distancing from Lady Catherine. I am sure they will have many more encounters in the future in which Elizabeth will have to hold her own. However, she does not feel threatened by her and wants to have a better relationship with this important family member.

Thinking and Feeling

One key to discovering the maturity of people, and their ability to have good relationships, is to observe to what extent their thinking and decision-making is governed by emotion rather than by facts. There is no question that we all are primarily emotionally directed creatures. We are all fused, inwardly and outwardly, to a certain extent. However, better-differentiated people are more able to distinguish between the emotional process and the thinking process. One process is not better than the other; the importance is that **knowing the difference between thinking and feeling gives us more freedom to act in the way we choose.** No doubt Elizabeth's emotionality is fired up and ready to fight Lady Catherine, as ours might be, but she is able to use the more rational thinking part of her brain to keep herself relatively calm and focused, and to just define herself rather than react aggressively to Lady Catherine.

Feeling-driven thinking is often driven by chronic anxiety. Thinking that is more rational is generally fact driven and guided by personally chosen principles and values that a person can consistently live by. This is not an anti-feeling idea. Better-differentiated people are quite good at recognizing their feelings and expressing them when appropriate. But they can choose whether to act on their feelings, restrain their feeling reactions when necessary, and know which direction is best.

People whose feeling and thinking are more fused together tend to be the ones with the most life problems. They have less ability to interrupt their automatic emotional reactivity. This affects nearly every aspect of their lives, especially their relationships. The more fused people are, the more vulnerable they are to stress, and the more symptomatic they will become, physically, emotionally, or socially. Lady Catherine is socially inept, and she gets away with her behavior only because of her aristocratic position.

Peoples' personal feelings are indicative of their subjective experience of their objective place in the emotional system they are a part of. You may be aware of how you feel differently depending on the group or the person you are with. As a Bowen theory therapist, **I never set out to change my client's feelings. When people change their objective position in a system, their subjective feeling experience changes automatically.**

Under the influence of fusion, we say, "you make me feel . . ." certain things, or do certain things, or be certain ways. We make others responsible for our feelings and actions. I might have said, early in my life, as a young man, to my wife, "You make me angry." She then would have said something similar back to me. We both had the sense that the other was creating our own subjective feeling ("*making* me feel . . ."), and then we would go back and forth, each accusing the other of creating our own reactions with how they were being. In this emotional fusion, we imply, "It is your fault that I am the way that I am. Who wouldn't act the way I do with a partner like you?"

In the more differentiated position, my feelings, just like my thoughts and behavior, are my responsibility. If my functioning depends on your functioning, then I am not able to act more responsibly, more independently, or with autonomy until you do. We think we can't change until the other person changes. This fused idea is what causes us to focus on changing the other person. Again, the issue of who is responsible for what gets all tangled up. **Better-differentiated people are responsible for self, not for the functioning of other people.** Other people, through their behavior, do indeed create the emotional environments (through what they do and say) within which we may have feelings, but our response to them is our responsibility. Lady Catherine certainly did create an emotional environment for Elizabeth and for others.

Differentiation and chronic anxiety are mutually exclusive. Elizabeth had to keep her anxiety tamped down in the encounter with Lady Catherine so she could respond appropriately out of her more solid, better-differentiated self. If she had been more anxious, they likely would have had a shouting match, with Elizabeth angrily telling off Lady Catherine for being the rude, self-centered, and arrogant person she is. That is what we may be tempted to do under such an onslaught.

We can be anxiously fused with those who disagree with us and, if so, we fight them. Rather than simply being people we disagree with, they become enemies. We have to defeat them and win the argument. Whatever principles or ethical beliefs we may have, say to love our neighbor, or to live like decent, civil, and kind human beings, or to be unselfish and giving, go out the window. We stop living by our professed principles. We start obsessively developing strategies to defeat "the enemy" or to win them over to our side. Both in families and in society, we know who to blame for the problems we experience, and we narrowly focus on those blameworthy people. It is harder for us to see the bigger picture. This describes much of the polarization in our society today. Both conservatives and liberals often act out of their fusion.

Solid Self and Pseudo-self

We are all part solid self and part pseudo-self. The more solid self a person has, the more differentiated that person will be. Solid self is stable and consistent. We base the solid self on our self-chosen values, beliefs, and principles for how to be in life and in relationships. The solid self is able to live up to the values it professes. It is not reactive to other people even if attacked. The pseudo-self is unstable and depends on what the social environment says, does, or expects of it. It is involved in the reactive processes of lending, borrowing, giving, receiving, trading, and exchanging of self.

Better-differentiated people work on having a more solid self. The principled I-position comes out of this. The solid self, in any given situation, says, "This is who I am, what I believe, what I stand for, and what I will and will not do." When Lois said she was no longer going to take responsibility for the relationship with my mother, that came out of her solid self. That action paid off for us both eventually.

Elizabeth is this kind of person throughout most of the story in *Pride and Prejudice*. In her early emotional encounters with Darcy, she has more of a fused focus on him and his personality. When she receives an important, clarifying letter from Darcy about some accusations she had made, she initially resists the truths it contains. At first she can't even read the letter because it presents facts that go against her emotionally based beliefs and prejudices. Slowly she sorts out her thinking and clarifies how she has failed to live up to her own principles of objectivity. She has not been the person she thought she was. She says she did not know herself. As she thinks her way through all of this, she becomes more rational and less reactive to him, a more solid self.

In this episode of Darcy's letter, **Jane Austen shows us how one works on self**, to become more solid, and that is what I admire most in her writing. We can see her heroes doing it; thinking their way through their turmoil. Elizabeth is able to focus on the facts of what has happened rather than maintaining her prejudiced beliefs about people. Without that kind of personal emotional maturity as a goal for her characters, Austen's wonderfully written sentences and her humor would have less special meaning for me. If Elizabeth had reacted to Lady Catherine as many of us might have, we might have cheered her on, but it would not have created change in relationships.

The part of us that participates in the fusion of the emotional system is the "pseudo-self." We call it "pseudo" because it is affected by how others want us to be, or how they are with us. Our fused self is the reactive part of us that is fused with others. For example, the compliant part of us might say, "We have to go along to get along." It knuckles under to the pressure to fit in with the goals and wishes of important others. Mr. Collins, in *Pride and Prejudice*, is an example of someone who lacks a solid self, as he shows by his compliance with Lady Catherine. In many areas of life, his goals are her goals for him. He even decides to get married because she has said he should. His livelihood depends on her approval, so he molds himself to what she wants.

This can happen in the fusion of a love relationship, where each partner may be willing to give up self to fit in with the wishes of the other, to keep the other close. Or they make emotional demands and threaten to leave unless the other conforms to their wishes. People in close relationships frequently trade pseudo-selves in this way, pretending to be what they are not, out of fear of losing the other. It is likely that each partner will do this to some extent and so, as Bowen says, "The two 'pseudo-selfs' fuse into a 'we-ness.'" Hall and Oates, in one of their songs, say, **"If two can be one/Who is the one two become?"**

Catherine Morland in *Northanger Abbey* is a good example. She gives up her self, her wishes, and goals in order to comply with the wishes of Isabella Thorpe and her brother. They ask her to lie to people she really cares about in order to do what they want her to do. When she goes along with them, she is operating out of her pseudo-self, the part that is emotionally fused. Slowly, Catherine is able to build up a stronger self and define her self to them. They get angry with her for this, but she can handle their anger and not react in kind.

The pseudo-self is the part that reacts to others. Over- and under-functioners both operate out of a pseudo-self. People in open conflict and rebels also operate out of a pseudo-self; for example, a rebel would focus on Lady Catherine's positions and say, "You can't talk to me that way! You can't do that to me. I'll show you. I don't care what you think. I can do anything I want and you can't stop me."

Self-Focus and Other-Focus

I want to make an important distinction here: Defining self, **becoming a more solid self, requires a self-focus rather than a relationship focus or other-focus**. I know this kind of talk makes us think of the personal ad that said, "Tall, dark, handsome Buddhist looking for self." We hesitate to talk about ourselves. We think, mostly correctly, that we shouldn't be so focused on ourselves that we exclude others.

Self-focus, as I am using the term here, is not self-centeredness or selfishness. **Self-focus is about the principle of "self-examination."** This is what Elizabeth does as she rethinks her relationships with Darcy and Wickham. She examines her way of understanding those relationships and, seeing how wrong she has been, concludes that, "I never knew myself." This means she failed to see that her own pride in being able to assess character was keeping her from seeing Wickham for what he really was, and that she has been prejudiced against Darcy.

Self-focus is about paying attention to how we function in life and relationships, particularly within the various emotional systems we are a part of. In our fusion, we tend to focus on how others function in relation to us, and what they want of us, or what we expect of them. We can be experts at the other-focus and do poorly with the self-focus. Maintaining an other-focus or relationship focus actually puts others in charge of us. In reacting to them, we abandon our own autonomy in relationships. Self-focus means regularly asking ourselves, "How am I doing at being the person I have set out to be? Am I relating to others in the way that I want to independently of how they are with me?"

Differentiation of self is automatic in all of us, up to a point; it is a normal part of growing up, and we don't become adults without managing it at some level. We don't have to understand Bowen theory to do it. Bowen theory just describes normal human processes that have always been going on, and it puts a name on them. We can all work at improving our functional level of differentiation and, as we do this, it will pay off in all of our relationships.

Dr. Bowen said:

Operationally, ideal family treatment begins when one can find a family leader with the courage to define self, who is as invested in the welfare of the family as in self, who is neither angry nor dogmatic, whose energy goes to changing self rather than telling others what they should do, who can know and respect the multiple opinions of others, who can modify self in response to the strengths of the group, and who is not influenced by the irresponsible opinions of others.

This is the major goal in life that all of Austen's heroes pursue. Fanny Price (in *Mansfield Park*) is an excellent example of a person who embodies the qualities described in the Bowen quote above. The novel shows us how she gradually overcomes her anxiety and becomes a better-differentiated person. Those heroes we admire the most in Austen's stories are the ones who emulate this behavior the best. In Austen's language, she focuses on her heroes being virtuous people of good character. Having these traits is not being able to profess them, or saying, "This is what I believe." To have character and to be virtuous in reality, to live according to the values we profess, requires having differentiation of self within the larger emotional system. This is the route to building character, living our professed values, and making better relationships.

Questions to Ponder

1. How would you think about your own level of differentiation? Can you give some examples that lead you to think you have correctly assessed your level based on the relationship between thinking and feeling in your life and how fused you may be with others emotionally?
2. Can you identify times when you have operated out of your pseudo-self?
3. What are some of the principles, beliefs, and values that you have developed on which you have based your life?

4. What are some examples of when you have failed to live up to these, and what are some examples of when you have?
5. In what ways have your levels of fusion and differentiation affected your life?

10

How Relationships Can Get Really Complicated: Triangles

The lower the levels of differentiation and the higher the levels of chronic anxiety, the greater the presence of triangling.

Peter Titelman

The word "relationship" is an abstraction. In its simplest form, a relationship is an emotional process that takes place between two people. As the two people attempt to engage each other in some kind of close relationship, they inevitably encounter differences in who they are and what they each want from each other, and in life generally. To have a good relationship, the two people have to have enough emotional maturity to negotiate their way through their differences.

This, in itself, can make achieving good relationships challenging. However, things are rarely this simple. For example, while it is no longer as big an issue as it used to be, a marriage between two people of different faiths could be a challenge. The wife may be a devout Catholic who relies on her priest to guide her in matters of faith and how to raise the children as Catholics. The husband may do the same with his Protestant pastor. Thus, the "relationship" is not just between husband and wife, but it also includes the priest and the pastor and their own faith beliefs.

Or the wife may have one or more girlfriends that she talks with about her marriage and the difficulties she is running into. The girlfriends have their own attitudes and experiences with "men" and are happy to advise the wife on what she should do or say with her husband in any particular situation. The husband also has his drinking buddies, and the topic of "wives" comes up with them frequently. They have their ideas about "women" and how to "treat" them.

In each of these examples, the husband and wife have to deal with what these third parties have to say about marriage and relationships as well as with each other. In Bowen theory, this is called a triangle. **Triangles are a major complicating factor to achieving good relationships.**

In chapter 35 of *Sense and Sensibility*, we have a dramatic scene that is brilliantly written and intriguing to read. Remember that Edward Ferrars and Elinor Dashwood clearly love each other, although neither one has openly declared this. The thing that stands in the way is that Edward, as a younger, foolish man became infatuated with the beauty of the young Lucy Steele and impulsively proposed to her. For several reasons, they kept this engagement quiet, and Lucy has confided the secret only to Elinor. Edward has not acknowledged it to anyone.

In that day, a man could not legally break off an engagement once he proposed, although the woman could. Edward is bound to Lucy, even though he does not love her. Lucy suspects his regard for Elinor and deals with this by cleverly taking in Elinor as her confidant, telling her everything. Her intent seems to be to warn Elinor away from Edward, relying on Elinor's discretion and honor not to infringe on her relationship with Edward. This strategy does indeed work.

In this scene, Lucy is visiting Elinor and celebrating her first visit to Mrs. Ferrars, Edward's mother. While they are talking, Edward arrives unexpectedly. He had intended to visit Elinor and had no idea Lucy was there. After he walks into the room and sees Lucy there, Austen writes: "It was a very awkward moment; and the countenance of each showed that it was so. They all looked exceedingly foolish; and Edward seemed to have as great an inclination to walk out of the room again, as to advance farther into it." This is exactly the kind of circumstance all three of them wanted to avoid. Lucy knows it is not her job to address the situation, and so she stays quiet. Elinor, in her maturity, is able to manage the uncomfortable situation the best.

The Concept of Triangles

What is going on here is the open revelation of a hidden triangle that has been going on through much of the book. Triangles are a common phenomenon in our lives. They are everywhere, and they are a part of nearly every relationship we have. If you watch soap operas on TV, then you are very familiar with triangles. They create much of the drama of these shows, just like in our own lives. Triangles are not just the sexual affair type, although a husband, wife, and mistress is one well-known type of triangle. Triangles test our level of differentiation and anxiety. Bowen said **the triangle is the basic building block of emotional systems** and of our social life.

The basic idea is that, just like a two-legged stool, **a two-person, one-on-one relationship can be unstable**. Stools need at least three legs to be stable. Two people in a relationship may get along just fine and be stable as long as there is no tension or anxiety between them. But as soon as one or both begin to feel enough anxiety, and the twosome cannot deal with it openly or directly, one or both will be tempted to turn to a third person.

Lucy is quite anxious about the future of her relationship with Edward because his mother may not approve of her. By confiding in Elinor, she is working on the triangular principle of keeping your friends close and your enemies closer.

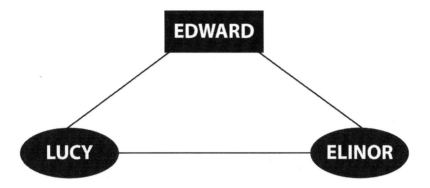

In this scene, there is a significant level of anxiety in them all, but Elinor is the calmest of the three. This allows her to function at a higher level of differentiation than the other two. Austen shows how she does this, and I will say more about this soon.

Just like real life, Austen's books are full of triangles. The above passage from *Sense and Sensibility* is from one of the classic ones. **The triangles usually involve some secret, where not everyone involved knows everything that is going on.** Here, these three people cannot talk openly and directly about what is going on, but the tension is there. Edward does not know what to do, or say, or even where to stand, literally. If you have seen the movie version of *Sense and Sensibility* (where Emma Thompson played Elinor), you may recall how Hugh Grant beautifully played Edward's awkwardness and uncertainty about what to do.

Once Elinor had learned of the engagement from Lucy, many people in her position would seek support in their sorrow by turning to someone else and telling them the whole story. That would add another triangle. For example, Elinor could tell her sister Marianne. If she had done this, Marianne, unable to contain secrets, would probably have told their mother or maybe even Mrs. Jennings, in which case the story would likely go all around their community since she is a major gossip. The number of triangles would have grown significantly. **Gossip is a common way we all create triangles.**

If the anxiety cannot be contained in the original two-person relationship, then triangles are a way that additional, vulnerable people (people willing to listen or become involved somehow) will be incorporated. If, for example, Elinor had told Marianne about the situation, Marianne would have immediately taken on some of Elinor's upset and anxiety. It is to Elinor's credit that, as a better-differentiated person, she does not need to seek Marianne's support and sympathy so she can feel better. She does not use the relationship with her sister to help her deal with her own anxiety.

Triangulation is a natural and automatic process in human society. **Simple triangles normally have two inside people and one outside person.** However, who is "in" and who is "out" can fluidly shift around. In the example below, Bill is unable to say directly to Ron what he thinks about Ron. That would involve some anxiety on his part, and maybe in Ron too if he heard what Bill thinks. So Bill is distant from Ron and talks to Jerry about Ron instead. Bill believes Jerry will be on his side and maybe have the same opinions about Ron. They are the close twosome and Ron is on the outside position.

However, Ron may also have some negative thoughts about Bill and will talk to Jerry about him. Jerry does not say to Ron what he and Bill have been talking about, but acts as if he agrees with Ron about Bill, who is now in the outside position. Then, sensing some kind of uneasiness with Jerry, Ron may talk with Bill about Jerry who does not tell Ron what he has said to Jerry about Ron, but acts like he agrees with Ron about Jerry. They are putting Jerry in the outside position.

The basic fluid triangle

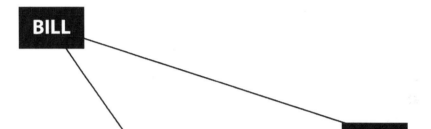

Confused? So are they. Everybody involved will have some kind of uneasiness, and they will be quite confused as to what is really going on. Part of Edward Ferrars's awkwardness and uncertainty about what to do is because he does not know who knows what. **If you feel confused about what is going on in a relationship, then look for triangles.** There may be some things going on that you are not being told about, and that will make you confused.

Talking about someone else who is not present in a negative way is triangular talk if you have not told that absent person the same thing, in the same tone of voice.

Here is a reliable rule: whoever talks to you negatively about someone else is just as likely, in different circumstances, to talk about you to someone else in the same negative way.

In the simple sexual affair triangle, a man may distance from his wife because of some kind of anxiety with her that is related to their differences. He may then go to another woman and say some version of, "My wife doesn't understand me like you do." Whether they become sexual partners or not, a triangle will exist. The husband and the other woman may or may not spend time talking about the wife, but she is a reality in the relationship. He feels more comfortable with this other woman because there is, *as yet*, no tension between him and her. She may also be married, and she will say to the man, "My husband is so dull and boring, and you are much more exciting." Since the original two married couples cannot deal with their issues directly and openly, it is much easier for them to talk with some other person. They feel better and less anxious, and the other person appears to understand what they are dealing with. However, if they become the primary couple, then as time passes, **the same difficulties will arise in their relationships**.

Of course, a triangle does not have to be an affair. The social triangle with friends (like in the example above with Bill, Jerry, and Ron) is actually the most common form of triangle. Lois and I live near a public walkway along the city's waterfront, and walking past other twosomes there, it is normal to overhear conversations. At least 70 percent of what we overhear is the two-some talking about a third person who is not present.

A (RON)

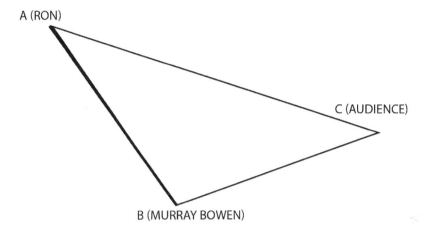

C (AUDIENCE)

B (MURRAY BOWEN)

Here is a triangle that you and I are part of right now: In this book, I, the author, could be acting as if I have the close relationship with Murray Bowen (or Jane Austen) and you, the reader, are in the distant position. I can act as if Bowen is always on my side—as if he agrees with me. Actually, all I am doing is giving you my version of Bowen theory. I can't really tell you what he thought; I can only tell you how I understand what he said. Many people go around claiming to be in a close twosome with some authority (Jesus is popular for some people) and act as if they and the authority are in total agreement.

You may know of some authority that you think backs you up on issues in your relationships with others. Perhaps you quote them whenever things get tough in the relationship rather than saying what you personally think. That is bringing in a third person for a triangle. Some of you may be quoting me to others, using me as the authority. Conversely, you may say to a close friend,

"Can you believe what he said!" putting me in the outside position. In either case, you may be misrepresenting my opinions so that they back you up. Since I am not there, I am not able to represent my own point of view.

Some triangles stay in the same configuration for years. Others are more fluid (Bill, Jerry, and Ron) and keep changing who is inside and who is outside. Sometimes you think you are permanently on the inside, and then you discover one day that suddenly you are on the outside. Someone has replaced you as the confidant that you thought you were to the other person. This happens to Elinor in *Sense and Sensibility* when Lucy reveals her secret to her. She thought she had the close relationship with Edward and is surprised to find out that she didn't. It doesn't feel good. It may hurt. You may get angry and want to get back at the one with whom you were once on the inside with. Things can really take off then: you may enlist others to take sides in a new triangle. Imagine what might have happened if Elinor had opened up to others about Lucy and Edward.

What causes triangles to form is tension or anxiety between two people that they cannot deal with directly and openly. Edward cannot talk openly and comfortably with either Lucy or Elinor. Elinor cannot talk to either of them about her feelings for Edward. This is one of the problems with triangles: because they involve secrets that are difficult to talk about openly, people are left wondering, "What is really going on here?" If Ron, Bill, and Jerry were able to say directly to each other what they were confiding in secret to the third person, they might still have differences with each other that needed to be addressed, but with absence of the triangling process they would have a better chance of resolving their differences.

One Purpose of Triangles

Triangles are there to absorb anxiety. That is why we form them. We want a friend to be supportive of us, to be on our side, in some other difficult relationship we have. While she has her strategic reasons for doing so, it is likely that Lucy Steele also finds some comfort in sharing her predicament with Elinor Dashwood. Elinor can share the anxiety about what will happen in the future. We think it will be comforting to find someone to share our secrets with, someone who will not condemn us or betray us. Maybe the person will agree with us or give us advice about what to do.

However, if we are more mature, we can avoid the triangling process ourselves. Like Elinor, this starts with managing our own anxiety in difficult relationships and working on our level of differentiation. **Better-differentiated people automatically do less triangling** because they are more comfortable dealing openly and directly with the people they have issues with. Or they can be comfortable dealing with the issue privately. They don't have to take their concerns to a third person.

From the moment Elinor learns of the secret engagement, she is the model of a better-differentiated person. Of course, she is angry and upset, but she is able to manage it well so that she does not make things worse for herself or, equally importantly, for Edward. She stays close to Lucy because she wants to learn the facts of the situation and understand it better.

We see that in this one scene where both Edward and Lucy are present with Elinor. Austen writes about how Elinor takes the lead within this triangular situation:

> And so anxious was she, for his sake and her own, to do it well, that she forced herself, after a moment's recollection, to welcome him, with a look and manner that were almost easy, and almost open; and another struggle, another effort still improved them. She would not allow the presence of Lucy, nor the consciousness of some injustice towards herself, to deter her from saying that she was happy to see him.

Less mature people, acting out of jealously, throughout the story would have tried to turn one of them against the other. This is what Caroline Bingley tries to do between Darcy and Elizabeth Bennet in *Pride and Prejudice*. The jealous person wants to separate the other two in the triangle. However, in this scene, Elinor does the opposite: "Her exertions did not stop here; for she soon afterwards felt herself so heroically disposed as to determine, under pretense of fetching Marianne, to leave the others by themselves; and she really did it." Elizabeth does something similar in *Pride and Prejudice* when she finds occasions to push Darcy and Caroline toward each other rather than try to separate them in a jealous way.

I have told of how my step-grandmother was jealous of my mother's relationship with her father. She worked hard to keep them apart. While she was physically successful in this, it only intensified the disregard the father had for his wife and the love he had for his daughter. When people feel insecure in this way, they often end up working against their own goals through this kind of effort.

Doing It Differently: Neutrality

Often, we are the recipients of secret information about someone else. We don't have to reject this overture, but neither do we have to collude with that person to form a triangle. Instead, we can be a resource. Because triangles are such predictable patterns, we can choose to behave differently in one even without knowing a lot about what has stirred things up. We don't have to talk endlessly with people about their complaints or concerns about others. In fact, it is not always helpful to do so. Talking more can gradually recruit a person into taking sides in the triangle, and while people feel good when someone takes their side, it does not really change things.

If you can talk with the person who has brought the secret to you or wants to talk in a triangular way, without taking a side for or against them in their difficulty, that is **taking a neutral position**. Let me give you an extended personal example. Remember, my mother was married four times. She ended all of the relationships except the last one with her husband Mike, whom she married after I had left home.

One of the reasons I kept my distance from my mother over the years was that I didn't particularly like the men she had in her life. I didn't want to talk with her about her relationships and complaints, and I didn't want to deal with my reactions to her choices in men. I might easily get angry at her for choosing them, and I didn't want to do that. I just preferred not to talk about it and keep my distance. I did complain to Lois about Mom's choices, creating a triangle with Ron and Lois in one corner and Mom and Mike in each of the other two.

Once I learned about Bowen theory and understood better what was going on, I was not happy about this situation. I wanted a better relationship with my mother and also with Mike. When I began to change the way I related to my family of origin, I knew I was going to have to deal with this basic triangular relationship, but without saying everything I thought about Mom's choice of men to her. I did not want to seem critical of her. On one of my trips down to Los Angeles, the three of us were going out to dinner. While driving to the restaurant, they began to argue heatedly about something that wasn't very important. This was typical behavior for them. I had all of those old feelings of wanting to distance, of not wanting to be there, wishing I could just get out of the car and fly back to Vancouver.

I knew that what I had to do was to move toward them rather than distance, without being judgmental and without taking a side in their argument, while also letting them know some of what was going on in me. So I hit on these words. When there was a break in their argument, I said, **"It really helps me to hear the two of you argue because I can understand better my arguments with Lois."** I did not say this with any intent of stopping them from arguing or getting them to work things out. I just wanted to get out of my silent, resentful distance from them. I was also acknowledging that I could be caught up in the same pattern, so I was not judging them.

The point of what I was doing was to get myself free from reacting to them, to be more neutral. That was my single goal. I was not trying to change their behavior. Doing that really worked for me. Because I repositioned myself in the triangle and became more neutral, my feelings changed. I felt freer and even somewhat warmer toward both of them (I no longer felt I was judging them), and even though it was not my intent, they calmed down significantly and we had a relatively pleasant evening at dinner. If you are in a similar position with someone in your life, my words will not work for you. What we say or do depends on knowing the principles involved.

I started doing one other thing in my visits to my mother and Mike that helped a lot with this triangle: I took charge of how I related to them. Being a resource in a triangle starts with the basic recognition of knowing what is happening. We can say to ourselves, "Aha! This is a triangle." Then we have to know that **A cannot change the relationship between B and C**. I could not make the relationship between Mike and my mother better, no matter what I did or how much I told them to shape up. However, I did have a one-on-one relationship with each of them, and I could change my behavior there

When I was alone with my mother or Mike and they started to complain to me about the absent partner, as they often did, hoping to get me to take their side, I did not say, "Hey, that's a triangle, and I don't do triangles. You are wrong to do that!" That would be judgmental, and they would feel put down. **I never point out triangles to the people who are trying to form one with me.** I just recognize it and decide to behave a certain way.

In addition, don't do what people often do in this circumstance. Either they take the person's side and agree with them about how "bad" and "wrong" the other person is, or they try to get the person to understand the other person's position. Both of these approaches put you on the other side of the triangle and will fail to change things between the other two.

At first, I dreaded how Mom or Mike would each complain to me about the other, but as I got free of my emotional reactivity to them and could be more neutral in the triangle, I could behave differently. I wanted to be a resource to the one who was talking to me without taking sides.

What I did is just what the best kind of friends do. They don't give advice or make suggestions; what they do is called "**taking a research stance**." They ask questions focused on the person who is talking to them. The intent of these open-ended questions is to encourage the person who is talking about someone else to think about their part in the relationship.

Let's say Mom is complaining to me about Mike. I will start asking questions about her behavior with him, not about him or his attitudes or actions toward her. She wants to talk about his "bad" behavior, but I show interest only in her. I ask her what she does in response to the behavior that she describes to me. I ask her about how she decides to act in the relationship at those times, in that way. **The point of the questions is to provoke more thoughtfulness about her part in the relationship.**

For example, after she describes something he has done, I ask, "What conclusion did you draw from him doing that? When you understand him that way, how do you tend to react? Do you think about how you would like to be in those situations? Is that the way you would most like to react? What has felt most helpful to you in the past in that situation? What do you think has been your best reaction? What made that your best reaction? Is that the way you would most like to be in those situations? Have you ever been able to do what you would like to do? Do you think that would help you get along with him better? What keeps you from doing that more often? What helped you do that when you did? Did it turn out that that was the best thing to do?"

There are literally hundreds of questions that could be asked. **Notice these are not questions with hidden suggestions in them** about what she "should" do. I am not inserting my beliefs or opinions about Mike, or about her, or about what I would do. With my questions, I am inviting her to step out of that fused feeling part of her and to *think* more about her relationship. I am inviting her to become more objective and see the bigger picture. People who give advice in these kinds of situations find that it is not taken, or the other person says, "Well, I tried that and it doesn't work."

Mom did make use of my questions. She did in fact start thinking more about how she was with Mike. In my subsequent visits, she spoke less about him in a complaining way, and she started volunteering more information about how she was with him and how she was deciding to live her life in relation to him. In response, I did not congratulate her; that would have put me right back in the triangle on her side. I just asked more questions. "What led you to do that? How did you happen to think about that? Did that help you deal with things in a better way? What made it better?" I could do the same thing with Mike when he complained to me about "your mother."

Bowen called this sort of stance "emotional neutrality." He also called it "emotional detachment," but people often misunderstood this as emotional distancing, which it is not. Being emotionally neutral means being detached from the emotionality of the situation. One can be both warm and emotionally neutral; this is a concept about objectivity, not about feelings per se.

In *Sense and Sensibility*, just look at how Elinor Dashwood functions throughout her acquaintance with Lucy in that triangle—it is fantastic. In spite of sometimes feeling quite anxious, she is able to be emotionally neutral with Lucy and not go into some sort of rage with her or Edward. She knows that Edward and Lucy will have to work things out between them, and she can do nothing about their relationship. She works at keeping a neutral relationship with them both.

This is what I did with Mom regarding her complaints about Mike. I detached myself from the emotionality and found a more neutral and less reactive position without taking a side. In addition, I saw how I had created my own judgmental feelings and was distancing from them both. This helped me understand what I had to do differently, so that the triangling process had a different outcome. This was a major change for me. I had been secretly very critical of Mom's choice of men for as long as I could remember, and this contributed to my distance from her. The change to a more neutral position was not easy for me, but it had a better outcome all around.

Mom did a better job of defining herself with Mike, and I saw some change begin to happen between them. My relationships with each of them were getting better, and they were fighting much less, according to Mom's report. Then, unfortunately, Mike died a premature death related to his heavy drinking.

Neutrality, or emotional detachment, involves keeping one's own level of anxiety as low as possible while staying in viable emotional contact with all of the important people in the system even as they disagree with one another. This is differentiating yourself within the triangle.

The neutrality has to be real; it can't be a strategy for getting a certain outcome. If you play favorites or secretly support one side against the other in any way, then the effort will fail. I had to achieve this kind of neutrality with both Mom and Mike. I had significantly different political beliefs and attitudes with Mike, and I had to get neutral about them. This neutrality is the essential element in what we call "detriangling."

This is the basic theory and method for being with friends while they are having conflicts with others:

- keeping in viable emotional contact with both sides;

- keeping your own anxiety as low as possible and not reacting to others;
- staying neutral and not taking sides; and
- maintaining the research stance, meaning asking genuinely curious questions that inspire others to think more about their situation and how they deal with it.

A calm tone of voice and a focus on facts is also essential. This is exactly what Elinor does with Lucy. She stays focused on the facts of the situation, not her feelings. This helps her maintain a mature position in the triangle. This kind of focus provides an atmosphere that others will appreciate and find useful, helping them to be more calm as well.

The more tension there is, the more active you will have to be in affirming your neutrality through your behavior. Don't say things like, "Don't expect me to take sides here. I am neutral." That won't cut it. People usually don't believe such statements, and the statement can even sound a little arrogant, like "I am above your petty problems." **We demonstrate neutrality in action more than in words.** An even bigger challenge is maintaining neutrality over the weeks and months, and perhaps even years, it may take people to resolve an issue, but it will pay off for everyone involved in time.

Questions to Ponder

1. Do you think you can explain the concept of a triangle to someone else? How would you do that?

2. What triangles existed in your family of origin while you were growing up? Are they now the same, or have they changed?
3. How have you been affected by triangles in your life?
4. Identify a triangle that is active in your life right now. How are you functioning within it? Are you happy with how you are functioning in it? Is there some way you would like to change your part in it?

11

Your Relationships

Can Improve

I only entreat everybody to believe that exactly at the time when it was quite natural that it should be so, and not a week earlier, Edmund did cease to care about Miss Crawford, and became as anxious to marry Fanny, as Fanny herself could desire.

Jane Austen, *Mansfield Park*

What have we now learned about what makes for good relationships? In my previous book on Bowen theory and Jane Austen (*Becoming Your Best*), I suggested that Austen might answer this question with, "Why of course, good people make good relationships." My earlier book focused on the "good people" part of that answer. It focused primarily on the concept of differentiation (discussed in this book in chapter 9) and the ethical implications of that concept in terms of personal character.

This book has enlarged the focus from the character of the individual person to the larger emotional system context of relationships. It is about the systemic challenges that can get in the way of becoming a well-differentiated person and having the best possible relationships.

Fanny Price: Showing Us How It's Done

Take the example of Fanny Price in *Mansfield Park*. Her story recapitulates the concepts in each of the chapters of this book. Like each of Austen's books, *Mansfield Park* is a case example of Bowen theory in action.

Of all of the Austen heroes, Fanny Price has the longest emotional distance to travel before she can have good relationships. We go on a trip with her in the book that is sometimes scary, upsetting, and extremely challenging for her. Her Cinderella-like life story might have turned out very badly. However, she not only endures the various difficulties she encounters, she grows through them to become a person capable of having good relationships.

Mansfield Park starts by putting Fanny in the context of her family system. The book begins as the story of the three Ward sisters. Due to their marriages (and their own character issues formed in their family of origin), their lives go in different directions. Their stories eventually merge back together, with the focus centered on Fanny. The middle Ward sister, Maria, is the first to marry, and she scores big in the marriage market. Mostly due to her beauty (and little else apparently), she attracts the wealthy Sir Thomas Bertram. Maria is mostly indolent and has few aspirations beyond living a life of luxury and ease, although she does have two sons and two daughters, who figure significantly in the story.

The oldest Ward sister, whose first name we never learn, marries a clergyman who ends up serving as the pastor in Sir Thomas's parish church. We know her only as Mrs. Norris. Her husband dies early on in the story, and that barely affects her life trajectory. Living up to her sibling position as the eldest, she is a major over-functioner, taking over much of the household management and parenting from Lady Bertram (Maria) who responds happily by under-functioning. Mrs. Norris is the one who suggests bringing young Fanny into the family as a kind of wait staff for Lady Bertram, relieving Mrs. Norris of that burden.

The youngest Ward sister, Frances, is Fanny's mother. Like many youngests, Frances rebels against the advice of others, and she chooses to marry the "bad boy." With an eventually disabled, heavy-drinking sailor for a husband and very little income to support their family of ten children, she is happy to let Fanny move to Mansfield Park. Fanny is their oldest daughter and, in many ways, along with her older brother, is the one who keeps the other children somewhat in line and organized.

Austen gives us a clear history for Fanny's difficulty with having good relationships. Without Austen saying so directly, I think that Fanny (and her brothers and sisters) was abused when she lived with her parents. Her father could be physically abusive, and her mother was inattentive to this. As with any physically abused child, this affected her sense of self and her confidence in herself. When she first moves into the "blended" Bertram-Norris household at Mansfield Park, she loses the leadership position she held in her own family. **She becomes an "exceedingly timid and shy" young girl**, "shrinking from notice." She is easily intimidated by authority and avoids any confrontation that could make people upset with her. She finds "something to fear in every person and place. She was disheartened by Lady Bertram's silence, awed by Sir Thomas's grave looks, and quite overcome by Mrs. Norris's admonitions." Even the maidservants "sneered at her clothes." **Her primary reactive pattern is to distance** from everyone except Edmund Bertram, who is always kind to her. Even with him, she is reluctant to be entirely open. She has difficulty saying what she thinks and feels.

Throughout the novel, we watch Fanny grow and become a more solid self. In chapter 23, we see her, for the first time, say what she thinks to Henry Crawford "with a firmer tone than usual." Then to herself, she thinks, "She had never spoken so much at once to him in her life before, and never so angrily to anyone; and when her speech was over, she trembled and blushed at her own daring." Fanny is openly defining herself to others.

In chapter 28, she first arrives at a kind of equal status to her cousins in the Bertram household, and maybe even ahead of them. At her first ball, given actually in her honor by Sir Thomas, she is dressed elegantly for her "coming out." She is to "lead the way" in the first dance and, "She could hardly believe it. To be placed above so many elegant young women!" In spite of continuing to be inwardly fearful and anxious, she is able to accept her new status with equanimity and truly to enjoy her new position in the family and in society.

Later on, "She was thankful that she could now sit in the same room with her uncle, hear his voice, receive his questions, and even answer them without such wretched feelings as she had formerly known." She is even able to ask about his business in Antigua, where he undoubtedly owns slaves. The anti-slavery movement was just then growing in England. This new strength with regard to him culminates in her ability to withstand Sir Thomas's demands that she accept Crawford's proposal of marriage and the vehement condemnations of her for refusing to do so. The whole family believes she is unreasonable and ungrateful for not accepting him. In spite of being in tears and feeling that "her uncle's anger gave her the severest pain of all," being all alone with no one to take her side, she remains firm in her refusal. She is clearly differentiating her self, not automatically complying with how others want her to be. Eventually, after Crawford runs off with one of Sir Thomas's married daughters, Sir Thomas sees that she was correct to reject him.

Slowly, Fanny learns to take principled stands with others, and to withstand the attacks and criticism from other family members. For example, they attack her for refusing to go along (the togetherness force) and be one of the group that enjoys doing the play. She manages to differ from Mary when Mary takes a critical stance toward Edmund becoming a clergyman. She eventually can hold her own in relationships and nonreactively say what she thinks. This improving level of differentiation on her part is a significant plus for much of the Bertram family. No doubt, with her marriage to Edmund, this influence will continue in the future.

Along the way, like other Austen heroes grappling with triangular forces, she has to deal with her jealous feelings as Edmund falls for Mary Crawford. She has to endure his praising Mary to her face when she knows that Mary is not the good person he thinks she is. His infatuation with Mary blinds him to her faults, and Fanny has to figure out how to position herself within this triangle without being overtly critical of Mary.

It takes Edmund some time to understand that the girl he befriended when they were both younger is actually the woman he would have the best relationship with. Before he sees this, he has to work his way through some of the relationship issues covered in this book to understand what would work for him in a marriage. He has to get beyond the many attractions of Mary Crawford, such as her beauty, cleverness, and worldly-wise ways. No doubt he would have gone far in life with her, but would he have been the person he wanted to be?

Fanny grows into a confident, attractive, and competent young woman of principle who, as we know, finally marries her cousin Edmund (it was not uncommon for cousins to marry in those days). She has loved him unwaveringly in spite of his attentions going to the enchanting and accomplished Mary Crawford. Mary and her brother Henry are relatives of Mrs. Norris on her husband's side. **Their character faults make them both unsuccessful in winning the partners they want.**

Fanny eventually becomes a leader within the Bertram household and becomes much cherished and increasingly appreciated by Sir Thomas. He became a better man and a better father because of her involvement in the family.

No one helps Fanny become a better-differentiated person. Just as is true with us, **this is work she has to do for herself**. No one can give her permission or do it for her. She considers the unreasonableness of her chronic anxiety, thinks through her own stance on things that are relevant to the family life, and then decides to risk saying what she thinks.

Fanny is quite dear to Austen. At one point, she refers to her as "my Fanny." At each step of the way, Austen shows us how Fanny manages to get some control over her life and become a significant person for others. Even though we have not lived her more difficult life, many of us can identify with her struggles.

Mansfield Park is not everyone's favorite Austen book. There are a number of difficult things to understand in it, like Fanny's attitude toward not participating in the play. To many people, Mary Crawford seems like a much more attractive person than Fanny, who can come off sometimes as a bit of a prude. Part of Austen's art in this book was to make Mary quite likeable. It took me more time to come to admire this book and Fanny, than the other Austen books and heroes. Many readers feel the same way, but I do now greatly admire what Austen has created in this book, and in Fanny.

Along with Catherine Morland in Northanger Abbey and Emma Woodhouse in Emma, Fanny has a significant distance to travel emotionally to

become a better-differentiated person and deal with the triangles that complicate her life. On the other hand, *Sense and Sensibility*, *Pride and Prejudice*, and *Persuasion* gives us heroes who are better equipped to deal with some similar challenges through being further along in their level of differentiation. This makes them capable of having better relationships all around, including with the man they marry. But although it takes Catherine, Emma, and Fanny longer to get there, each of these women shows her ability to maintain an open and equal relationship with the man she marries.

In addition, all of these heroes choose men who can appreciate their strength of character, who are open to hearing what they think, and who value their ability to relate as equals. We have little doubt that they will make good marriages. They will be good family members and friends to those they care about.

The I-Position Contributes to Good Relationships

When we finally realize that we can't change others while the mobile of family life is anxiously spinning out of control, taking a more differentiated I-position within the system is a way to stabilize things. Like Elizabeth Bennet with Lady Catherine, we can become a more solid self and say, **"This is what I will and will not do."** That one private encounter between just those two women had ramifications for both the Bennet and Darcy family systems. If one person can stabilize themselves, then others may be able to do so as well. No doubt even Lady Catherine will grow and change through this process.

The I-position involves taking responsibility only for one's self, not for the others in the system. This is a major challenge within any emotional system. Fanny could only be responsible for herself, even when others were not being responsible. When things are going crazy in a system, we are prone to tell others to "calm down." That usually does not work so well. We can only do that for ourselves.

Elizabeth Bennet does not say, "Lady Catherine, you are out of control; you need to be more composed." Usually, we say something like this when we are more fused with others and think that their upset is upsetting us. We think if they could be calmer, then we could be calmer. That is because of fusion in the emotional system. Lady Catherine would be impervious to such a comment. It would not change her. She would just be more reactive and upset. Instead, we ourselves have to be calm and that is what others may catch. Anne Elliot's calmness in the emergency at the Lyme Regis Cobb, when Louisa falls and nearly dies (*Persuasion*) is a great example of how this works. It impresses even Captain Wentworth, who has himself become somewhat frazzled by Louisa's accident.

At critical times in an emotional system, when just one person is functioning in a more differentiated way, especially around some emotionally loaded issue in the system, their actions are not always applauded by others in the system. As when Fanny refuses to act in the play, or to marry Henry Crawford, **others often diagnose**

them as "stubborn," "selfish," "uncaring," and any number of other negative terms. They apply these labels to anyone who does not comply with their togetherness-force-based wishes.

Lady Catherine is an excellent example of this reactivity in her condemnation of Elizabeth Bennet for refusing to promise not to marry Darcy. Central, more fused people may make whatever threats they think will bring others into line, "If you don't change and give up this crazy thing you are doing, I will never talk to you again." Or, "I'll write you out of my will." Remember, in *Sense and Sensibility*, this is exactly what happens to Edward Ferrars when he refuses to give in to his mother's demands: she disinherits him. In *Emma*, because Frank Churchill fears his parents, he keeps his engagement to Jane Fairfax a secret.

A further example of the I-position occurs in chapter 58 of *Pride and Prejudice*. Darcy and Elizabeth are coming toward each other with openness about themselves instead of making accusations, as they each have done in the past. Each one admits that they had to work through their own emotionality and be able to think about how they themselves had behaved. She explains, "How gradually all her former prejudices had been removed." He talks about how his own feelings are "so widely different from what they were." They have each repositioned themselves in their triangles, and now their feelings are different. **They are no longer focusing on the other but only on themselves and whether they are living up to their own standards.**

Here is a contemporary example of taking an I-position. A woman I knew insisted on inviting to her wedding a side of the family that her parents (her dad especially) had long been cut off from and wanted nothing to do with. This distance came from an old feud that went back to issues with her dad's parents. Her dad berated her for inviting them and said he would not walk her down the aisle and that he and his wife would not come to the wedding if these relatives were there. These were, of course, heavy emotional threats for her, but the woman calmly and nonreactively said, "They are a part of my family, and I want them at my wedding." She said, without anger, "Dad, you know how much you and mother mean to me, and how much I want you involved in my wedding, and to help celebrate my marriage. These relatives are also a part of my family and I want them to come as well. Please continue to be a part of my wedding even though I am going to invite them."

Up until a few days before the wedding, her parents kept saying they were not coming, and they participated in the wedding preparations only minimally. The daughter did not react and get angry with them. That would be acting out of fusion. She maintained her I-position. She continued to relate warmly to her parents and spoke openly with them about whatever was going on with her wedding plans. She did not plead with them or try to get them to understand her position by explaining her thinking to them repeatedly.

In the end, her parents did come to the wedding. Her father did walk her down the aisle, and her parents behaved well with the estranged members of the family at the reception. In fact, they appeared to enjoy each other; they could not remember the exact reasons for the original conflict, and made plans to see each other again.

This woman's differentiation of self took a high level of courage. It eventually had a positive impact on her family—though she did not do it for that reason. **We do not differentiate our self within the emotional fusion in order to help others grow, but that is the frequent outcome.** Courage to be able to maintain our position even when under attack, without being reactive, while also maintaining our connection with those who are reacting is a critical part of the differentiation process. The paradox is that differentiation of self leads to growth and to creating better relationships.

Openness and Vulnerability in Relationships

One of the goals of Bowen theory is to be able to establish a one-to-one relationship of closeness with important others. This means each person can say what they think, feel, and want to do or have done, with regard to themselves or the other person, without fear of the other's reaction (even if the other reacts negatively). Whenever the other also engages in this kind of openness, the person can listen, understand, and not react. This is what Austen shows us in her heroes, and what my friend did around her wedding.

Most of us are not willing to let ourselves be fully known, to say who we are and what we think and feel, unless we feel safe with the other and can "trust" them not to attack us. We want them to accept us before we open up. Many relationships cannot get past this point.

People remain guarded and closed. The trust never develops, and so people fail to be open and vulnerable. **When we have developed a mature enough self, we don't wait for that trust to develop.** Instead, we trust ourselves to be able to handle whatever the other comes at us with. We don't need their permission, or cooperation, or their guarantee of acceptance before we tell them who we are. This is the way my friend approached the wedding invitation with her dad.

We don't get to the open, one-to-one relationships until someone is willing to take that risk and be vulnerable. They have developed enough confidence in self to do this. They trust themselves enough to be able to handle whatever might come at them from the other. A good place to work on this kind of emotional growth is with our own family of origin. If we can do it there, with those emotionally important people, with an awareness of the kind of issues covered in this book, we can usually do it anywhere.

My intent in this book has been to show that achieving good relationships is more complicated than the usual "Ten Steps" approach in popular psychology self-help books. It is not that these books are wrong, but it takes a broader, more comprehensive approach to relationships to see all that is involved. **I have described here what it takes to put into action what the other self-help books suggest.** Bowen family systems theory gives us the needed perspective to achieve this.

Along with describing Bowen theory and showing how Austen illustrates it, I have told you about my own development. As I worked at improving my relationships with my family, especially my mother, using the insights of Bowen theory, my marriage improved as well. This makes sense because my more distant and insecure way of relating began in family. It was not easy for me (in fact I found it quite scary), but as I changed my patterns of relating in my family, I developed the skills for a better relationship with Lois. She also did similar work in her family and we both grew as a result.

The better-differentiated person is more able to be aware of the thinking and feelings of others and to tune in to what is going on with them. A better-differentiated person can listen well to the thinking of others, asking many questions about how they arrive at their own conclusions and how they sort out the issues for themselves, without needing to change them or their thinking. **They can be aware of the feelings of others without feeling impinged on by those feelings.** The others will appreciate this interest in them that is not focused on changing them.

I will give one final example of my improving relationship with my mother. For most of her life, she had experienced questions as a kind of "nosiness" that she did not appreciate and tended to react to. I have spoken about my reaction to her apparent lack of interest as she lived out this philosophy as a parent. However, gradually, she became more comfortable with my "nosy" questions and I became more comfortable asking them. Our relationship began to improve as she became more willing to tell me about her life and respond to my interest.

On one of her visits to Vancouver, I asked her if she would be willing to make a video tape of me interviewing her. I said I wanted to show the tape to my trainees in the counseling training program I directed. The intent was to show how to interview a parent. With some reluctance, she said yes.

In the video interview, I asked her many questions about her life, her growing up, and decisions she made. For example, at one point I asked, "How do you account for your four husbands?" Without hesitation she said, "I was always looking for the love I didn't get from my father." We had talked about a lot of the background of this statement before, so I knew something of what she was saying, and about how she ended up distant from her father. Now she was clearly able to put her adult relationship difficulties with men into the context of her family of origin.

Later in that same interview, talking about something that was not very emotionally heavy, Mom began to cry. She had never cried in front of me, ever. I knew this vulnerability was a big deal. I said, "Mom, can you tell me what the tears are about?" She said, "I so wish I could have talked like this with my father." She burst into sobs. Here was an emotional issue that she had lived with all of her life, that she had never been able to openly address, and that was deeply involved in her difficulties with having a good adult relationship with men, and with me.

This was a breakthrough moment for both of us. We had done a lot of work to get here. **In the years leading up to this moment, we had both worked at becoming more open**, and she had already been changing how she related to Mike.

As she herself moved toward death, lying in her nursing home bed, she said, "I know I should be asking you some questions, but I just can't." She had not been able to change that basic pattern in her life, but just commenting on it was a change. I said, "That's fine with me, Mom. When I have something I want you to know, I'll just tell you." She smiled and said, "Good." I have tears just as I tell these stories here.

She died not too long afterward. I was so grateful that I was able to be closer to Mom over the preceding years. We had both moved slowly toward this point. In my first ever, real face-to-face talk with her about these things, she helped it happen. I wrote to her to say I was coming to Los Angeles for a conference and I would like to come a day early and spend it with her one-on-one. I said we could drive down to Laguna Beach (where we had our first holiday together in LA), and I would like to ask her some questions. She said okay. Up to that point I had only asked questions through the mail, not face-to-face. Face-to-face seemed like a big deal to me.

I picked her up early in the day in my rental car, and we spent much of the day driving around, talking about inconsequential things. About two hours before I was going to drop her off at her home, she said, **"I thought you had some questions to ask me."** I had been avoiding this moment of us sitting and talking face-to-face about personal stuff. I had never done this before in person and I was scared. I said, "Right. How about we stop here at this restaurant for some drinks?" I actually trembled physically, as I sat talking with her in a way I never had before. It went well, and she said, as I dropped her off, that she would like to do it again. We were on our way!

A couple of years later, after more visits like this one, she called me to say that she was going to leave Mike. This surprised me, since we had never talked about this possibility before. I said I could come down and help her move out of the house, which I did. While I stayed neutral in that triangle with her and Mike (whether she should or shouldn't leave him), this occasioned further conversations, and my questions then helped her to think more about her relationship with Mike and how she managed herself with him. She began to think about how she could be different with him, and after a few more months, she decided to move back in with him. This was a change, since she had been ready to write him off, divorce, and move on as she had done in her other three marriages. Their relationship improved somewhat after that.

I made similar efforts with other family members, and my relationship with each of them improved as well. As they each died, I was able to be present and accountable, as the only family member available, to help them at the end. Before doing this work, there is no doubt that I would have disappeared on them.

Dr. Michael Kerr, who took over as director of the Bowen Center after Dr. Bowen died, wrote: "The higher the level of differentiation of people in a family or other social group, the more they can cooperate, look out for one another's welfare, and stay in adequate contact during stressful as well as calm periods." This statement accurately describes the kind of people Austen's heroes represent and what they, through their own maturity, contribute to their family and relationship life.

This approach to improving relationships does not need the cooperation of others to be effective. As one person in a relationship works at his or her own level of differentiation, their relationships will improve just by virtue of that person behaving differently. Others may well catch on to this themselves and start making changes, but that is not the focus of our own work.

I hope I have inspired you to work on your own level of differentiation and to see the usefulness of the other concepts in this book. If you do, there is no question that your relationships will improve. I am forever grateful to Bowen theory for opening up to me how relationships can improve, and to Jane Austen for giving me some heroes to admire who have done this work themselves. I have tried to convey to you how it can work in your own life, and hope you have found it useful.

Appendix I

A Brief Biography of

Jane Austen

Jane Austen was born in a small community in southern England, at the end of 1775. Her father was the Reverend George Austen, and her mother was Cassandra Leigh. As the seventh of eight children, she had only one sister (her lifelong best friend) who was three years older than Jane. She also was named Cassandra. Two of her brothers rose through the English naval ranks to become admirals. One became the Admiral of the Fleet for Britain. Another brother was adopted out of the family to be the child of wealthy, childless family friends named Knight. He maintained his connection with his birth family and, after the father's death in 1805, was able to provide housing and support for his mother and two sisters, who had a very small income.

Jane had less than two years of formal education. Her highly literate family was supportive of her home-based learning and of her creative writing, which began when she was a young girl. Her father had a large library, and her reading in both fiction and nonfiction was extensive.

She was highly social and loved going to neighborhood parties and balls. She was most enthusiastic about dancing. She had at least two love interests, but for various reasons, they did not go very far. In one case, a young man's family brought him back to Ireland because they did not think her social status was comparable to his. He became the Chief Justice of the Supreme Court of Ireland. In his nineties, long after she had died, he said that he had been in love with her. She remained unmarried to the end of her life. She had accepted one proposal, but by the next morning, she had changed her mind.

Jane left a number of short stories and poems, known as her juvenilia, written when she was quite young. Her more mature and better-known novels were a product of her young adulthood. She had finished her first three novels, *Northanger Abbey*, *Sense and Sensibility*, and *Pride and Prejudice*, by the time she was twenty-one. There were two unfinished novels: *The Watsons* (which she abandoned writing during an eleven-year period of low productivity in her life), and *Sanditon*. She was working on it when she died.

She died in 1817 of an undiagnosed disease that is commonly thought today to be Addison's disease. That disease is treatable today. She was forty-one years old. She is buried in Winchester Cathedral in southern England.

Appendix II

Jane Austen's Family

Jane Austen family diagram

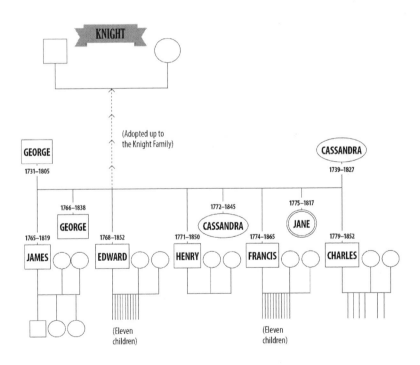

Appendix III

Family Diagrams for Each Novel

Northanger Abbey families

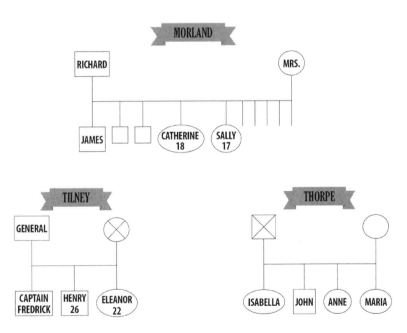

Sense and Sensibility families

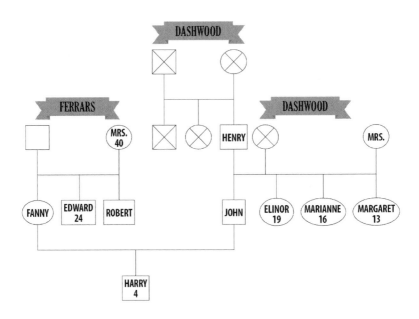

Pride and Prejudice families

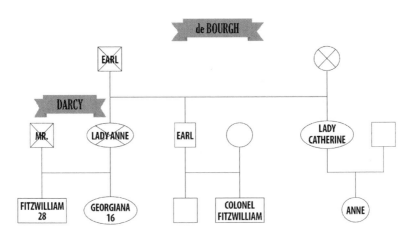

Pride and Prejudice families

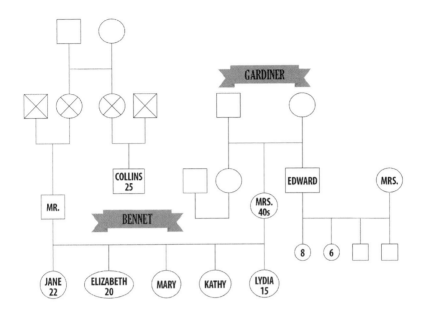

Emma families

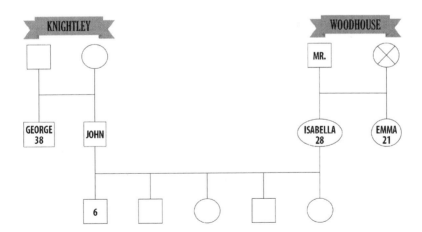

Mansfield Park families

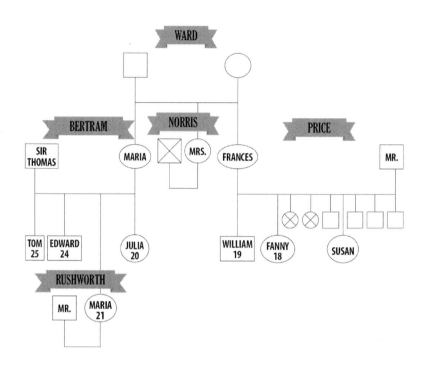

Persuasion families

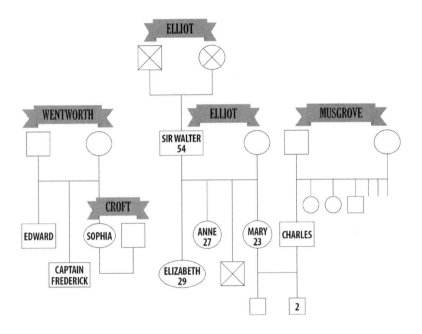

Appendix IIII

Counseling and Training

Opportunities in Bowen Theory

Bowen Center for the Study of the Family
Washington, D.C. www.thebowencenter.org

Bowen Family Systems Clinical Seminars
Prairie Village, Kansas phone: 913-722-1010

Center for Family Consultation
Evanston, Illinois email:
info@centerforfamilyconsultation.net

Center for Family Process
Washington, D.C. www.centerforfamilyprocess.com

Center for the Study of Human Systems
Falls Church, Virginia www.hsystems.org

Center for the Study of Natural Systems and the Family
Houston, Texas csnsf.org

Clergy Seminars
Whitehall, Michigan www.clergyseminars.net

CSNSF Border Programs
El Paso, Texas border.csnsf.org

Des Moines Bowen Family Systems Theory Study Group
Des Moines, Iowa phone: 515-288-8000

Family Health Services
Houston, Texas email: vaharrison@sbcglobal.net

Florida Family Research Network
Delray Beach, Florida email:
ebgfamilycenter@adelphia.net

Healthy Congregations
www.healthycongregations.com

KC Center for Family Systems
Kansas City, Missouri www.kcfamilysystems.org

The Leader's Edge
Potomac, Maryland coachingleadership.com

Leadership in Ministry
www.leadershipinministry.org

Your Mindful Compass
Washington, D.C. email: arms711@aol.com

The Learning Space
Washington, D.C. phone: 202-966-1145

Living Systems
North Vancouver, BC, Canada www.livingsystems.ca

New England Seminar on Bowen Theory
Dorchester, Massachusetts email:
annvnicholson@gmail.com

The Prairie Center for Family Studies
Manhattan, Kansas www.theprairiecenter.com

Princeton Family Center for Education
Princeton, New Jersey www.princetonfamilycenter.org

Programs in Bowen Theory
Sebastapol, California programsinbowentheory.org

Southern California Education and Training in Bowen
Family Systems Theory
Chula Vista, California www.socalbowentheory.com

Vermont Center for Family Studies
Burlington, Vermont
www.vermontcenterforfamilystudies.org

Western Pennsylvania Family Center
Pittsburgh, PA wpfc.net

Workplace Solutions
Burlington, Vermont www.workplacesolutionsvt.com

Made in the USA
San Bernardino, CA
28 September 2017